WITHDRAWN

SAN DIEGO PUBLIC LIBRARY
NORTH PARK

WAR-FIX

Also available in this series:
Silk Road to Ruin, $22.95
Johnny Jihad, $9.95
P&H: $3 1st item, $1 each addt'l.

We have over 200 titles,
write for our color catalog:
NBM
555 8th Ave., Suite 1202
New York, NY 10018
www.nbmpublishing.com

ISBN-10: 1-56163-463-8
ISBN-13: 978-1-56163-463-7

Book design by Steven Olexa
printed in Singapore

3 2 1

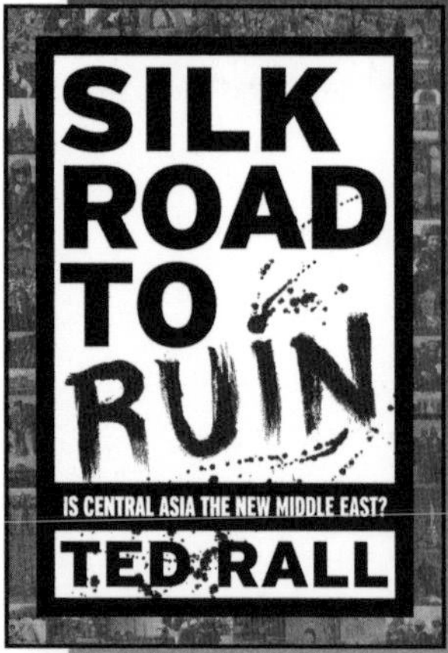
SILK
ROAD
TO
RUIN
IS CENTRAL ASIA THE NEW MIDDLE EAST?
TED RALL

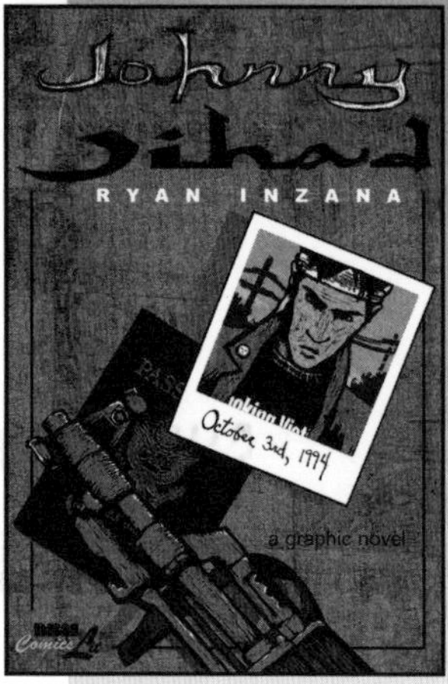
Johnny
Jihad
RYAN INZANA
October 3rd, 1994
a graphic novel

ComicsLit is an imprint
and trademark of

NANTIER • BEALL • MINOUSTCHINE
Publishing inc.
new york

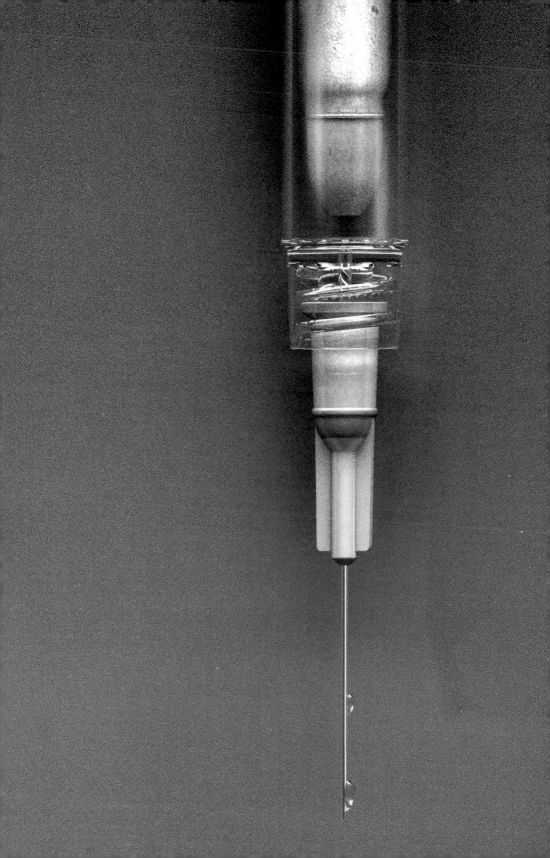

STORY / ILLUSTRATION
DAVID AXE / STEVEN OLEXA

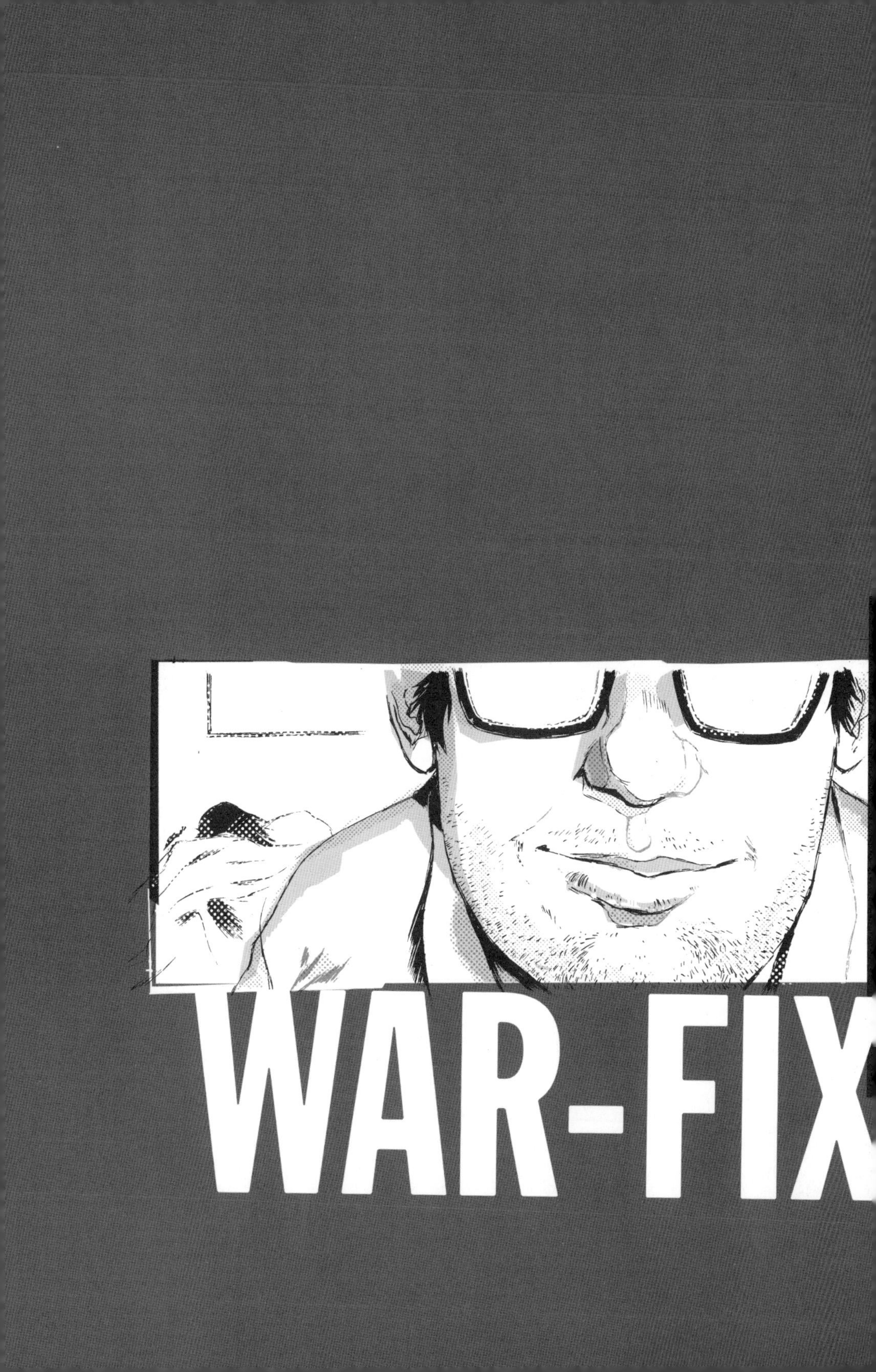

WAR-FIX

JANUARY, 1991

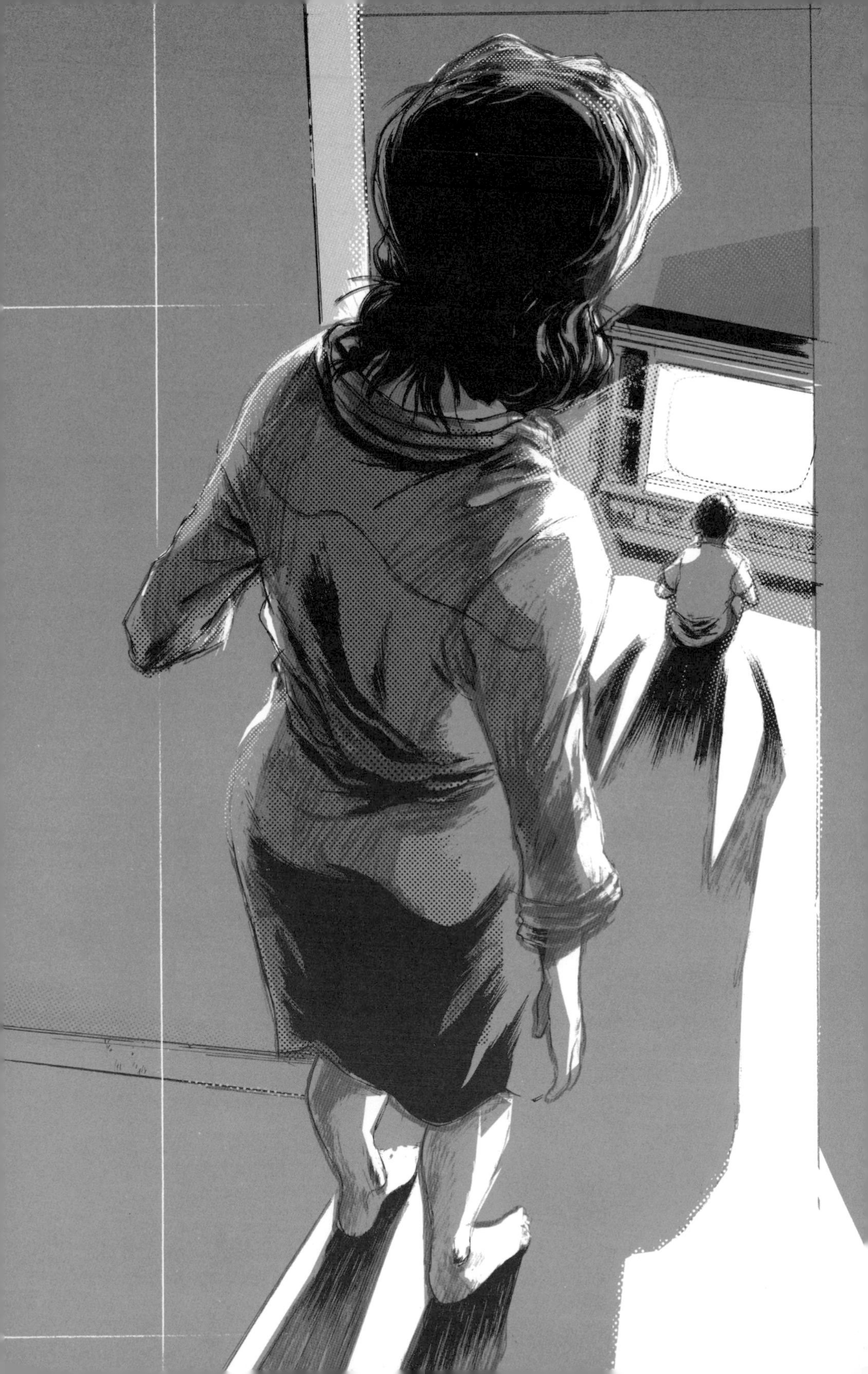

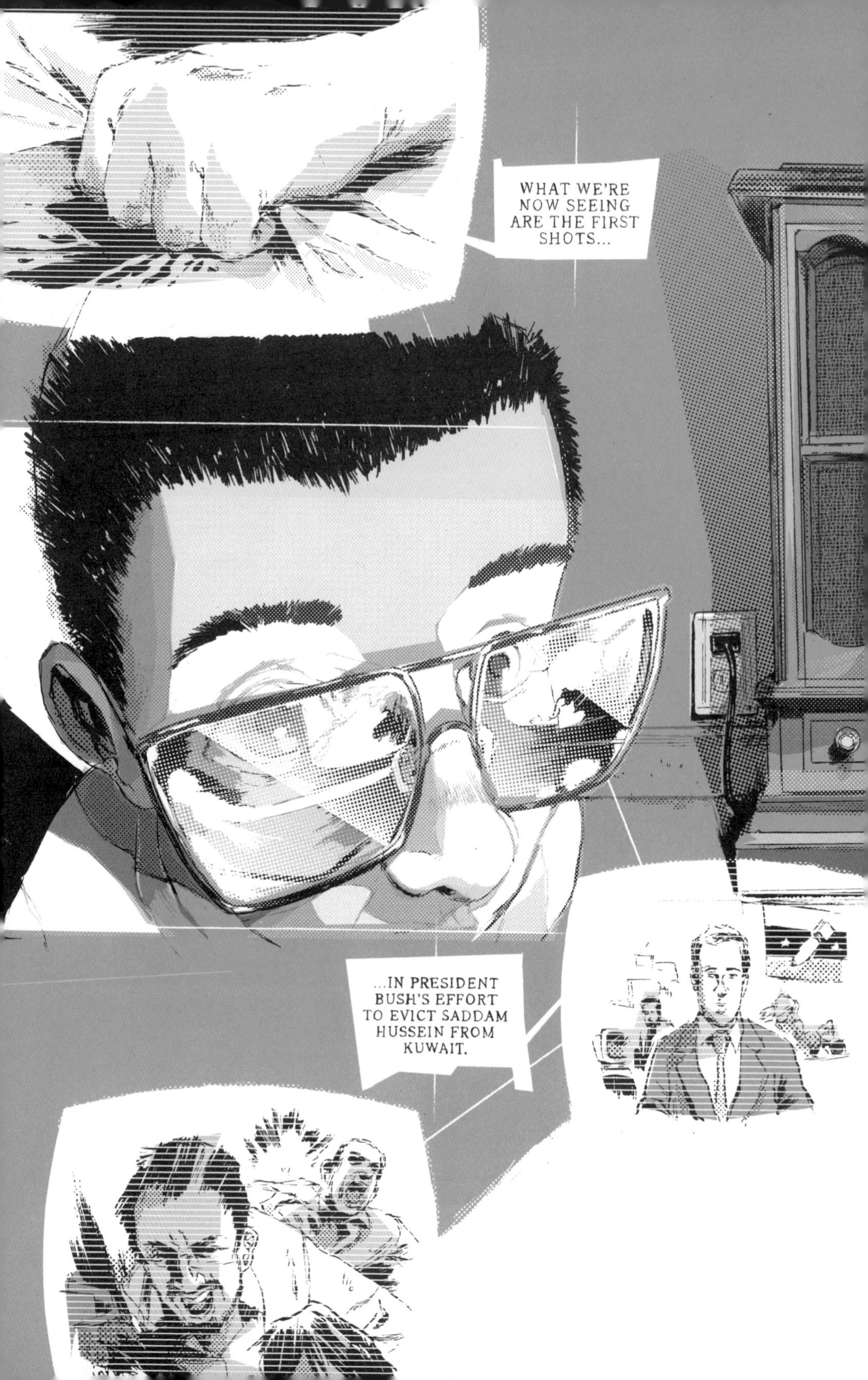
WHAT WE'RE NOW SEEING ARE THE FIRST SHOTS...
...IN PRESIDENT BUSH'S EFFORT TO EVICT SADDAM HUSSEIN FROM KUWAIT.

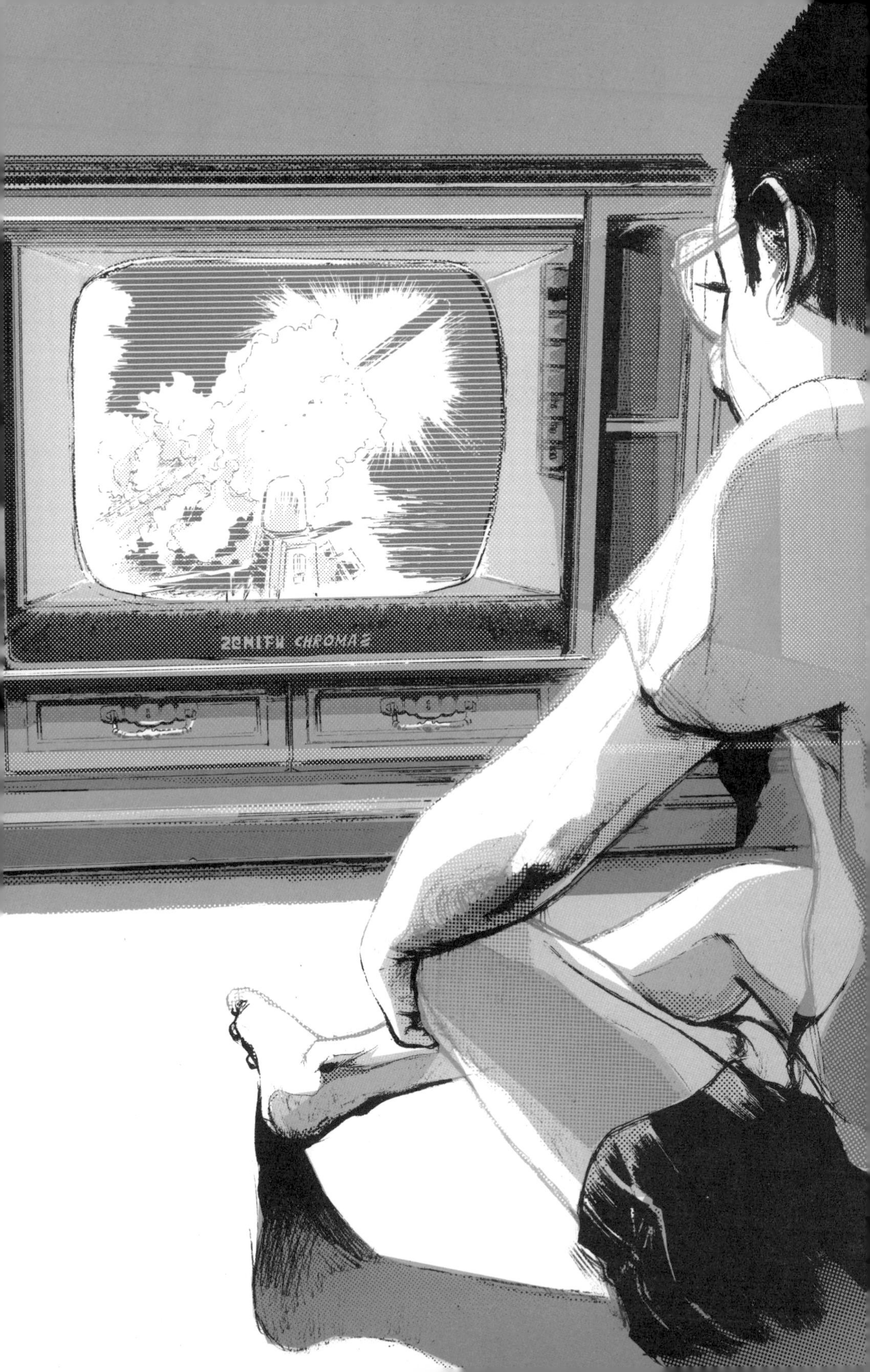
ZENITH CHROMA

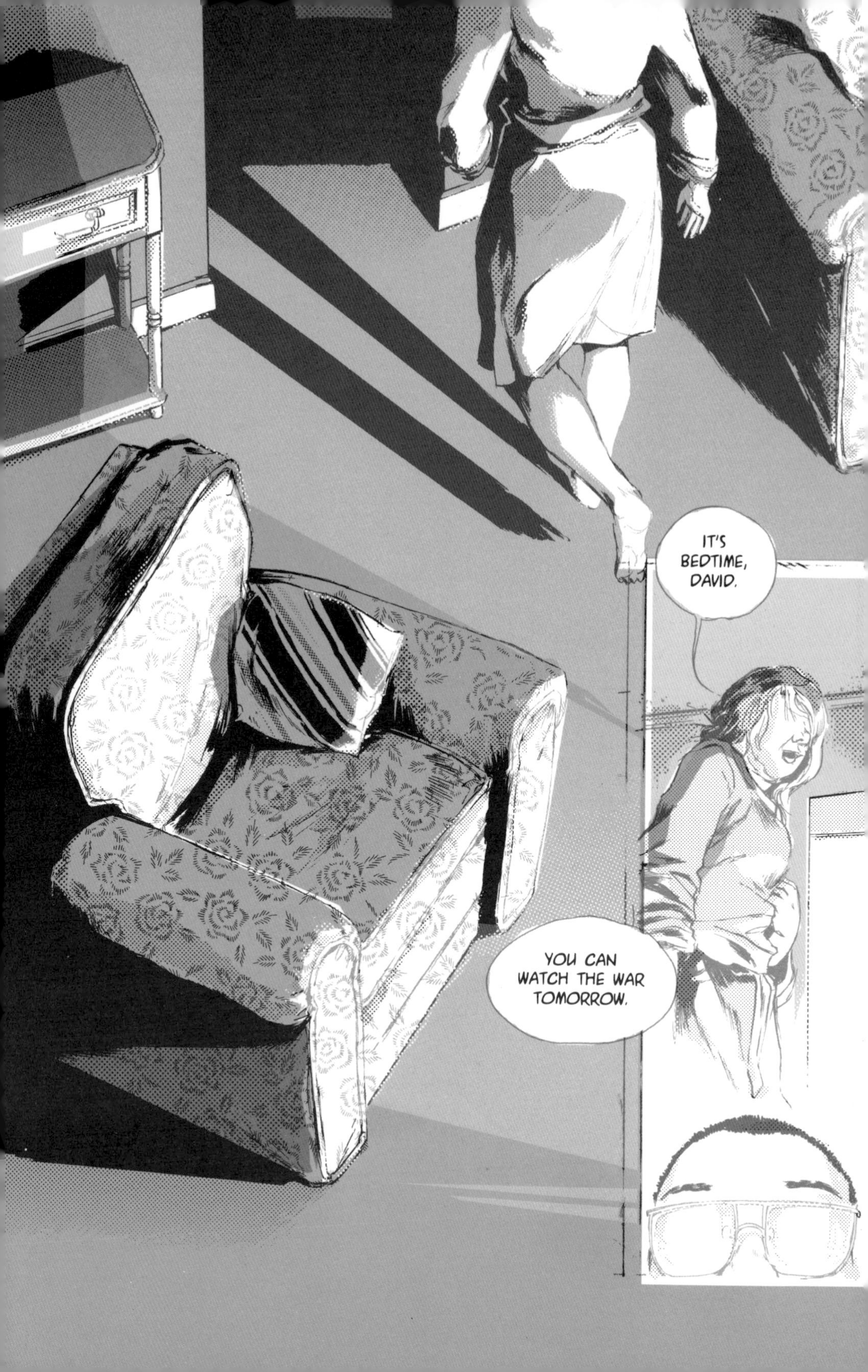
IT'S BEDTIME, DAVID.
YOU CAN WATCH THE WAR TOMORROW.

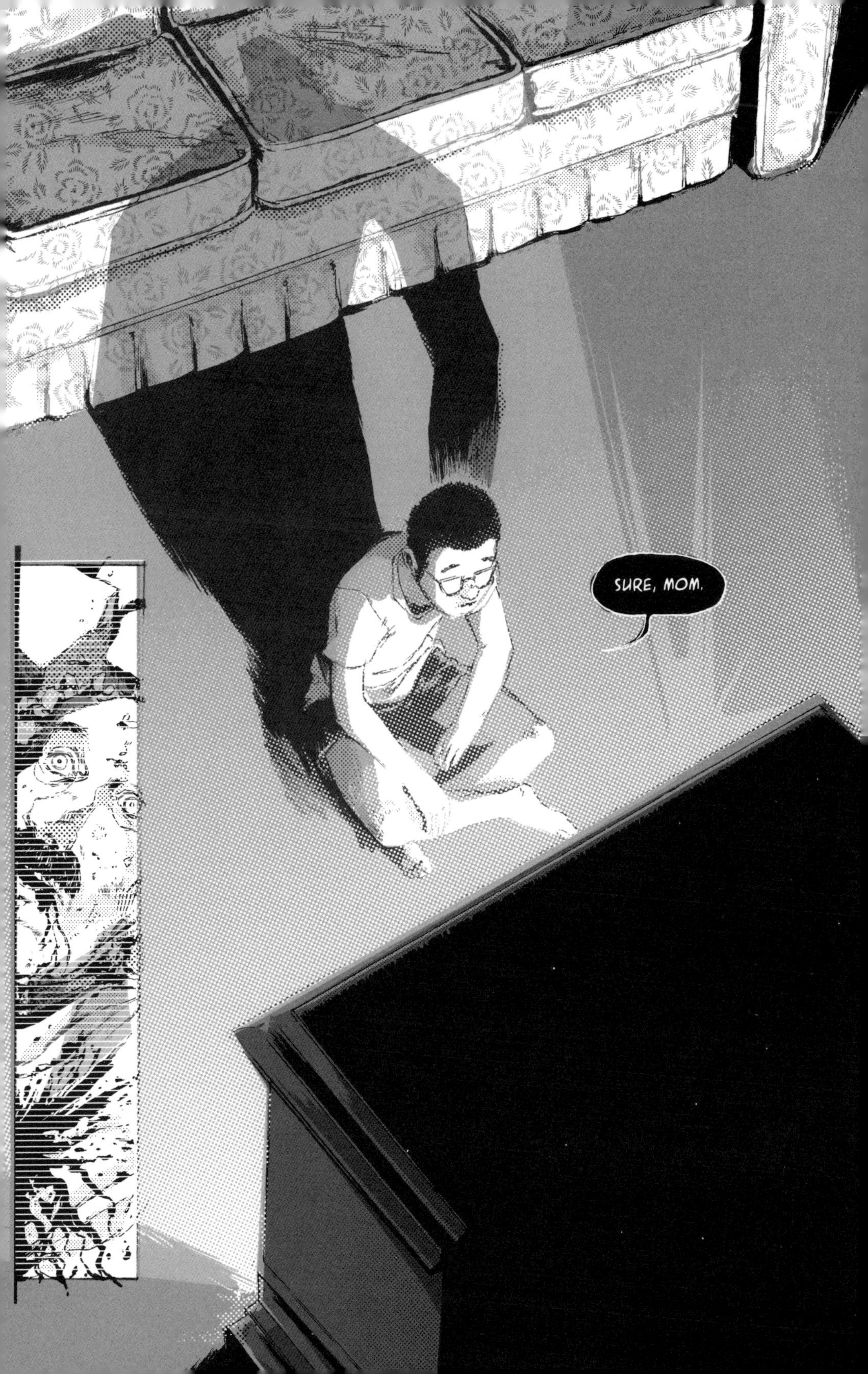
SURE, MOM.

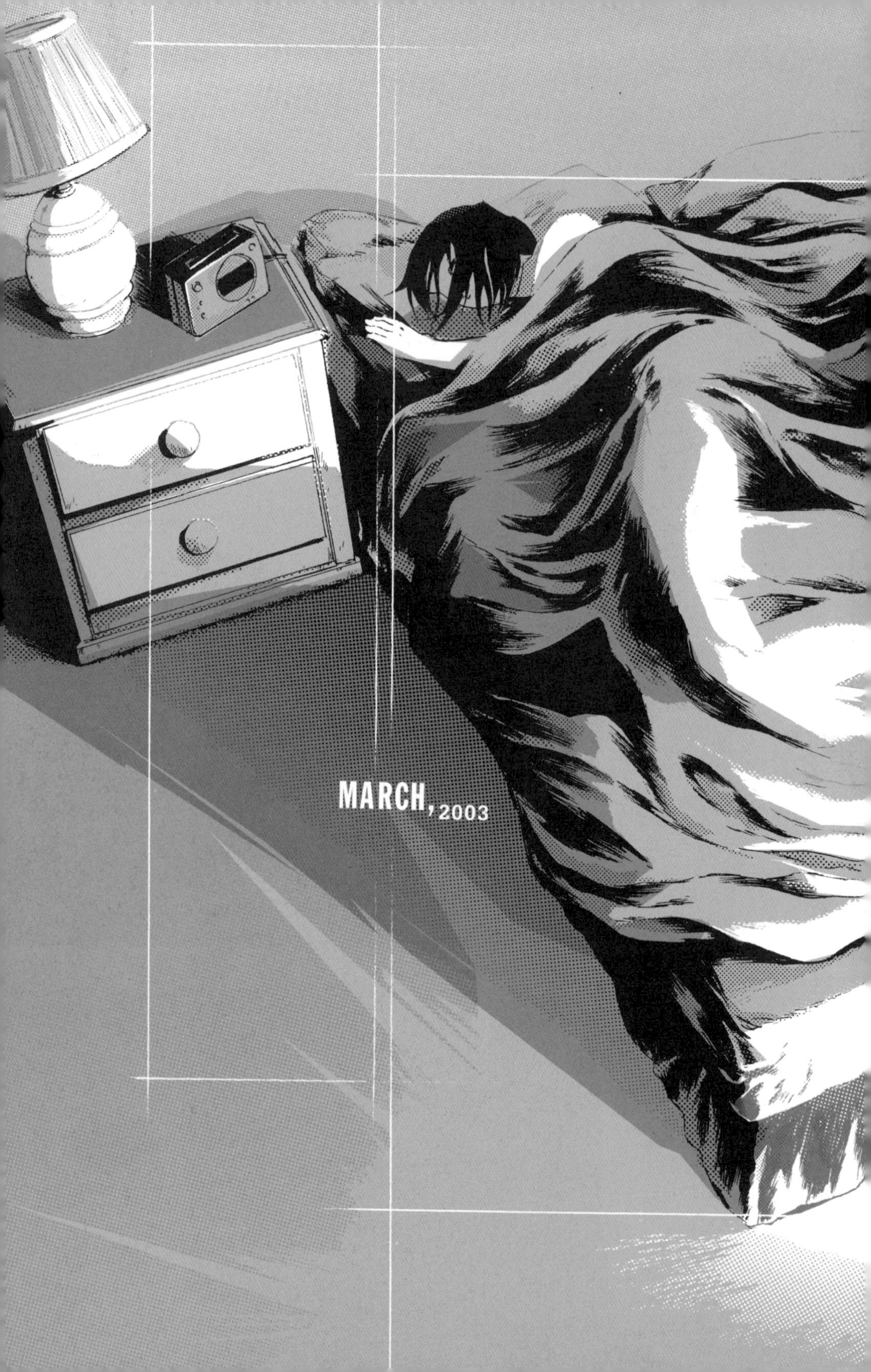
MARCH, 2003

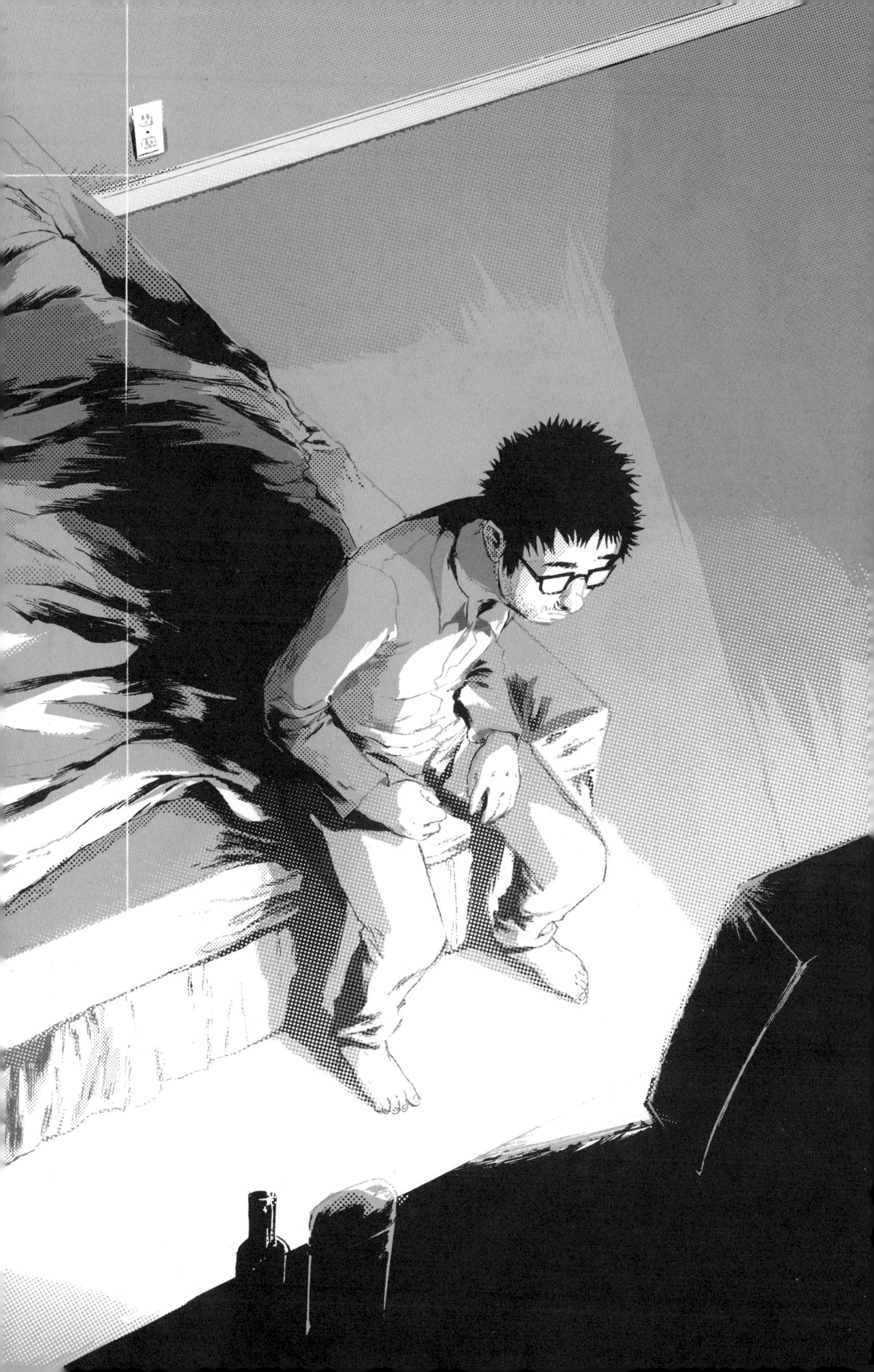

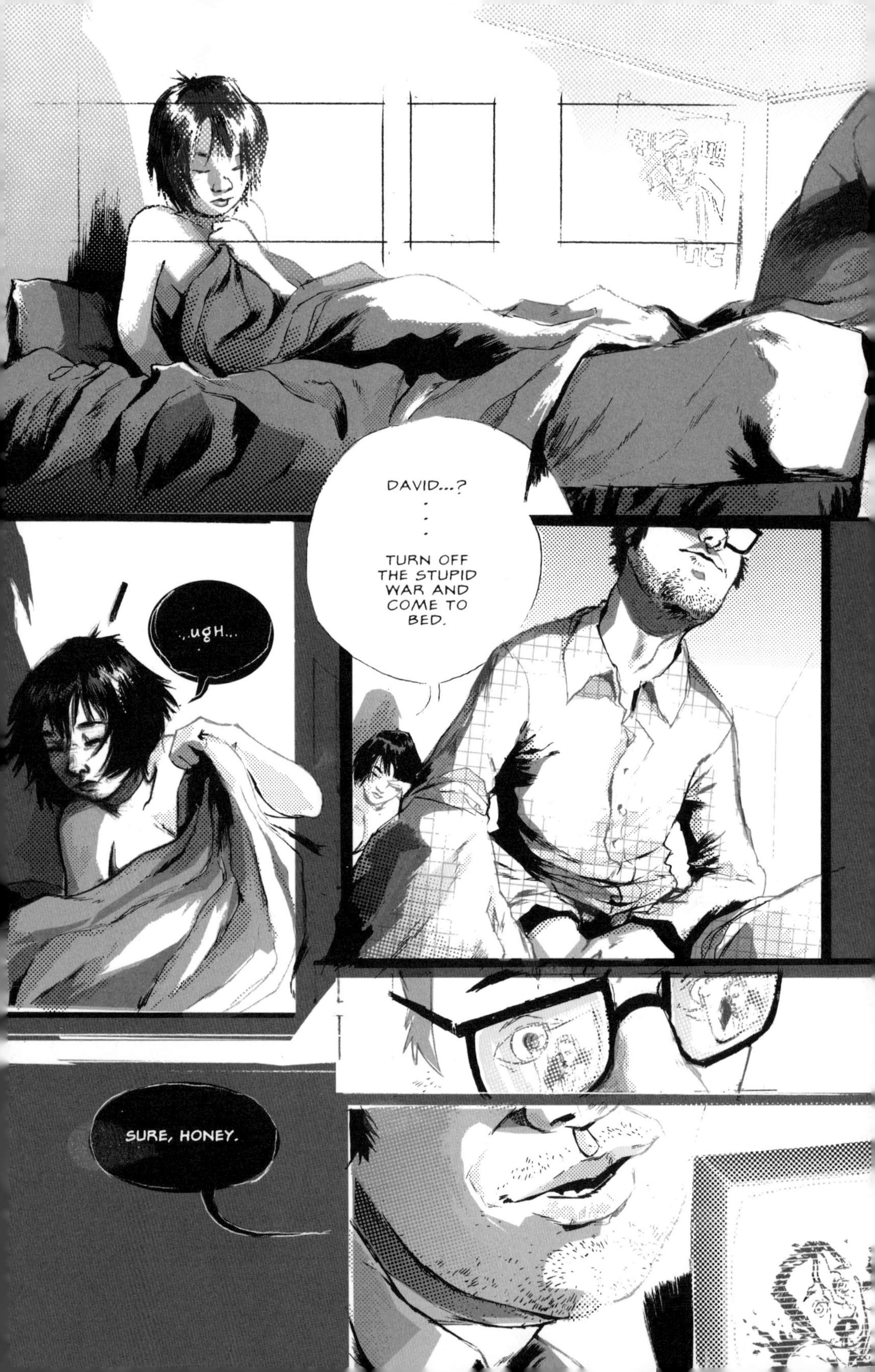
DAVID...?
. . .
TURN OFF THE STUPID WAR AND COME TO BED.
..ugh...
SURE, HONEY.

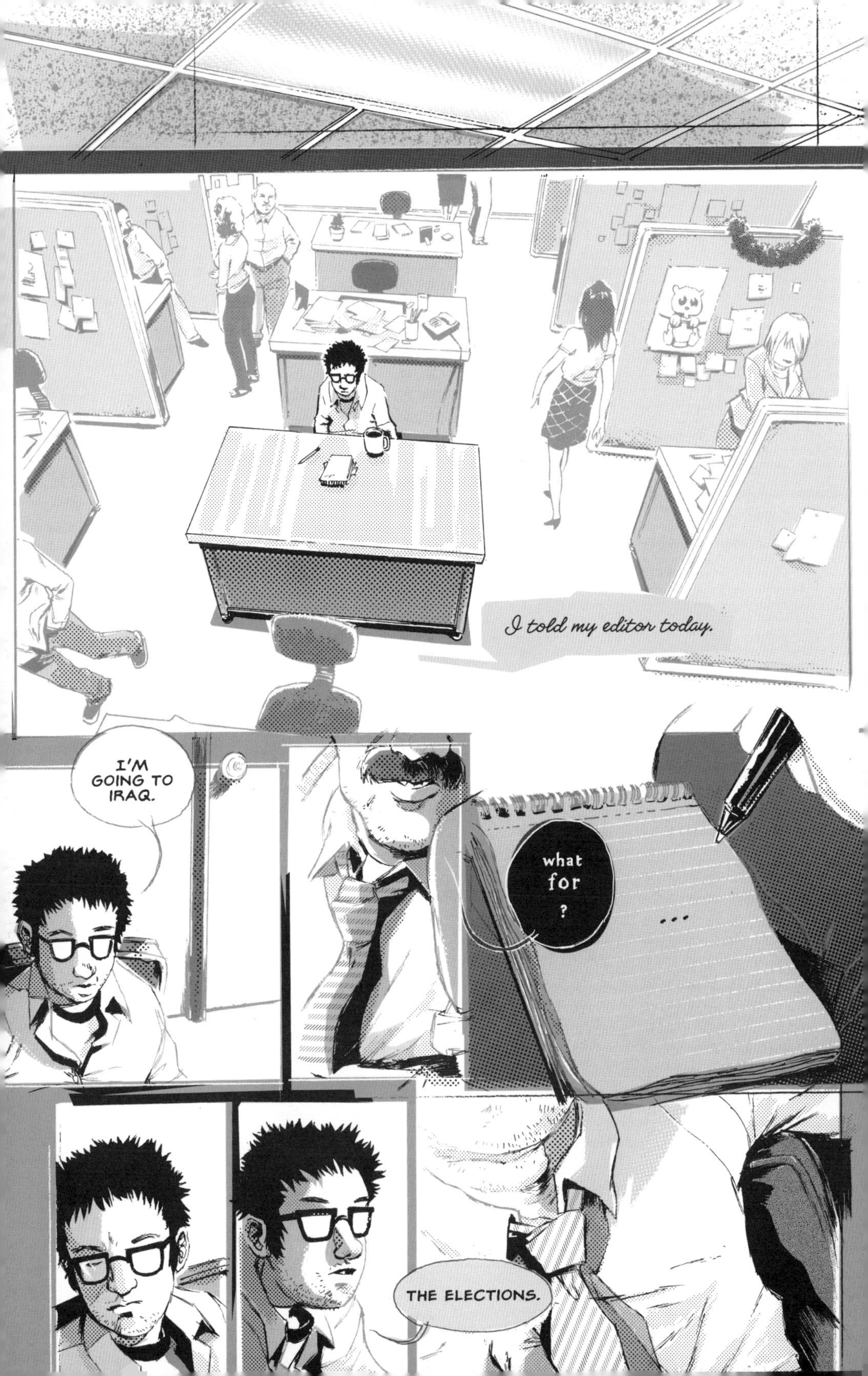
I told my editor today.
I'M GOING TO IRAQ.
what for ?
...
THE ELECTIONS.

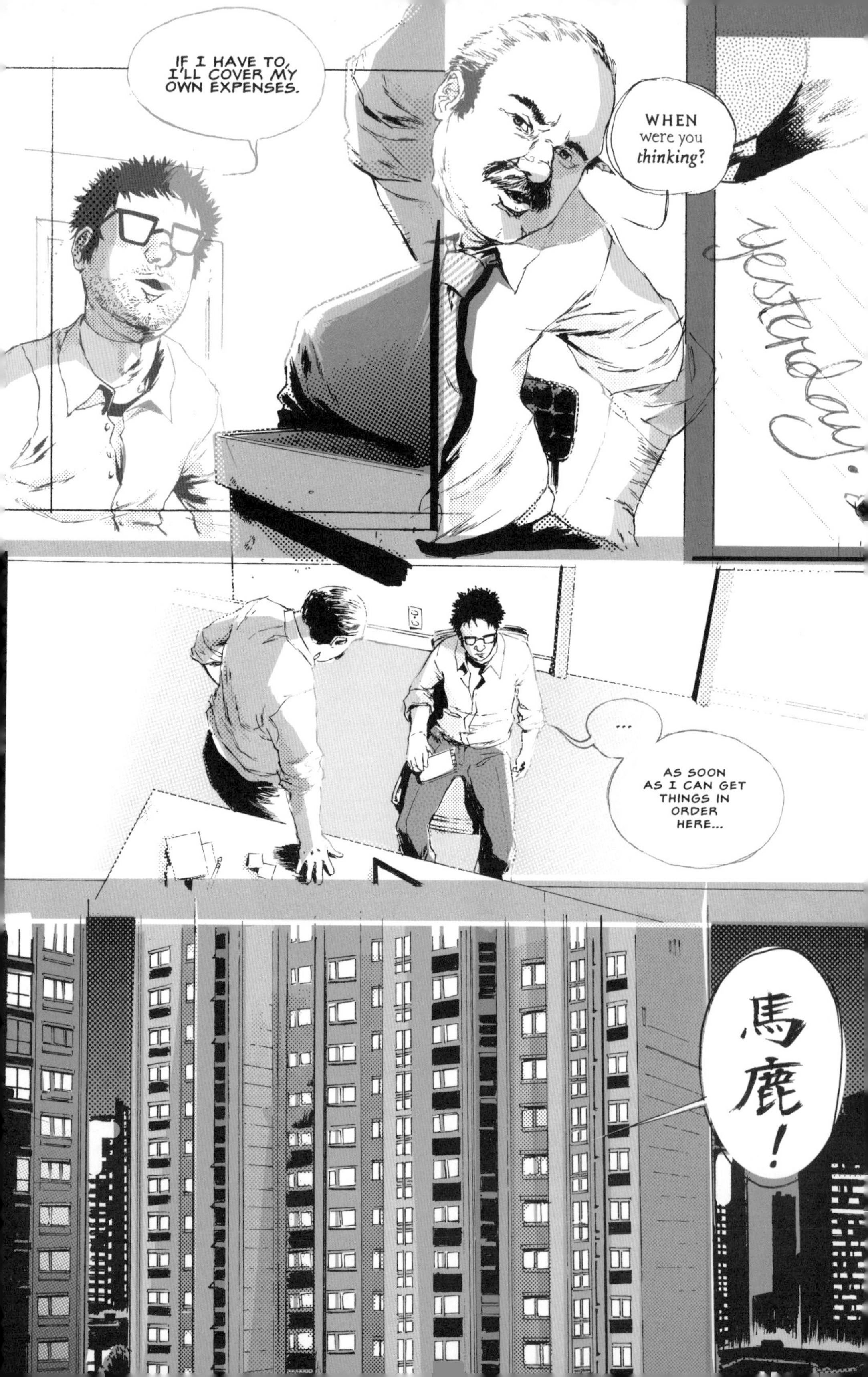
IF I HAVE TO, I'LL COVER MY OWN EXPENSES.
WHEN were you *thinking*?
yesterday.
...
AS SOON AS I CAN GET THINGS IN ORDER HERE...
馬鹿!

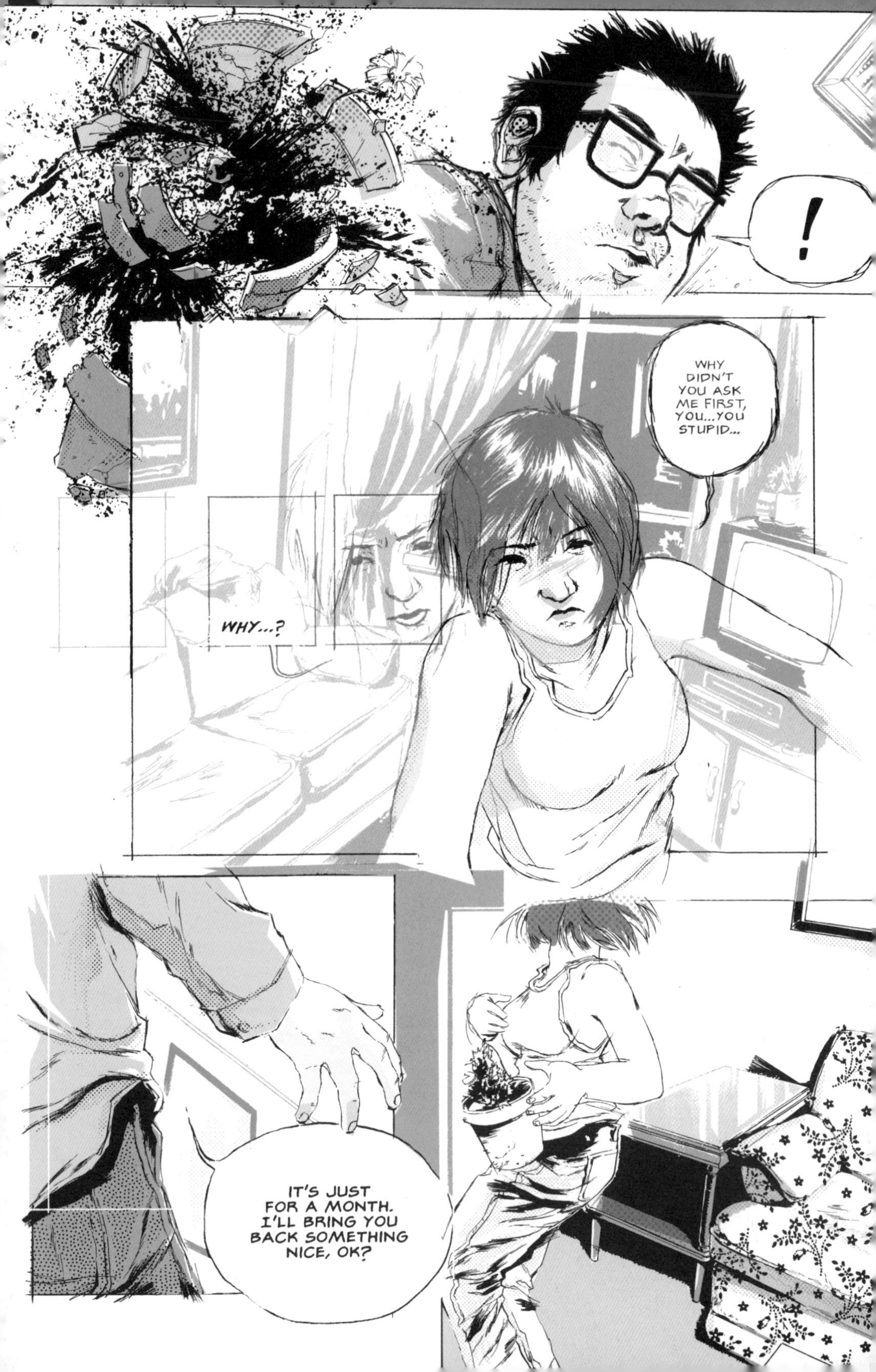
!
WHY DIDN'T YOU ASK ME FIRST, YOU...YOU STUPID...
WHY...?
IT'S JUST FOR A MONTH. I'LL BRING YOU BACK SOMETHING NICE, OK?

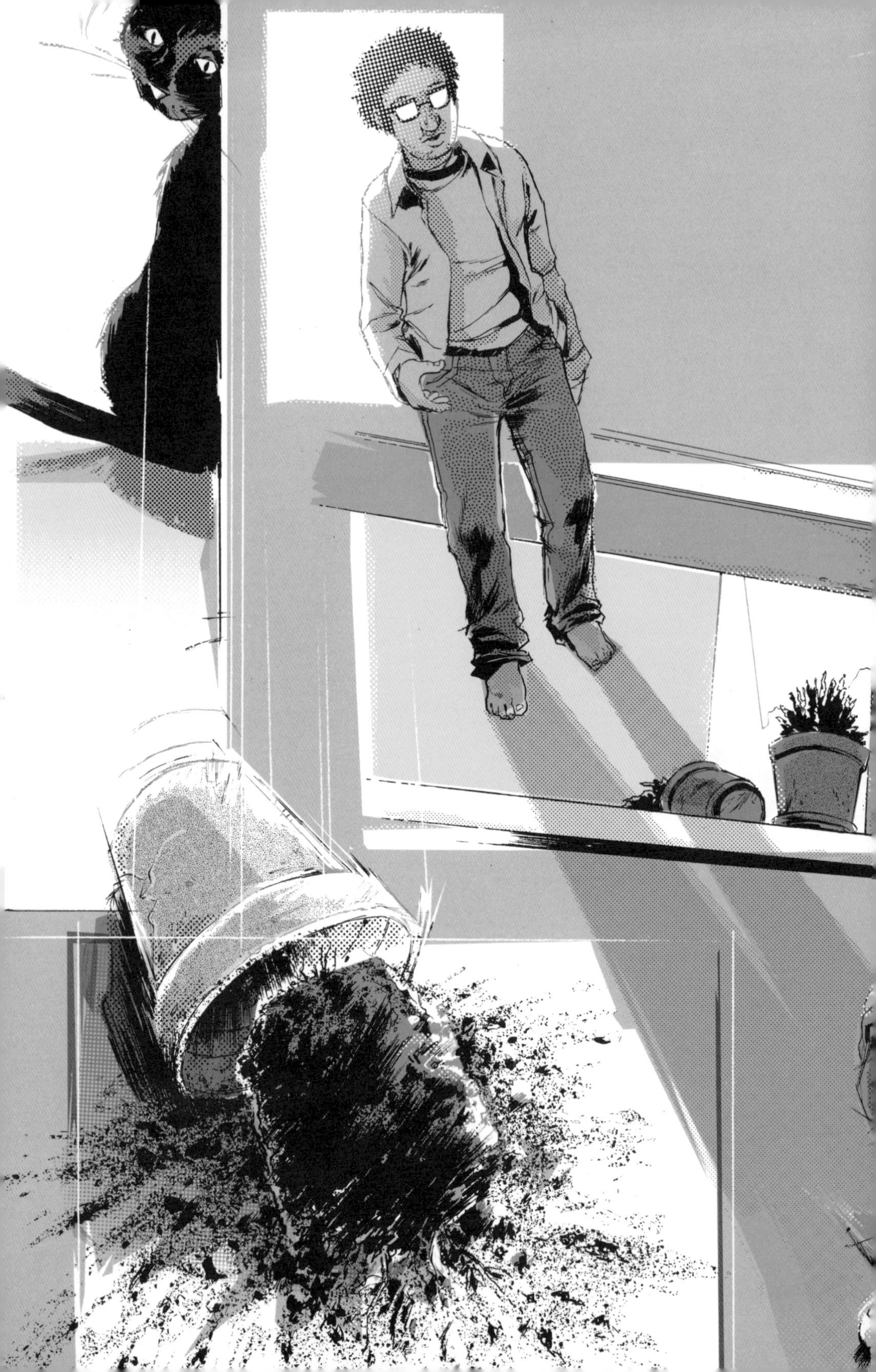

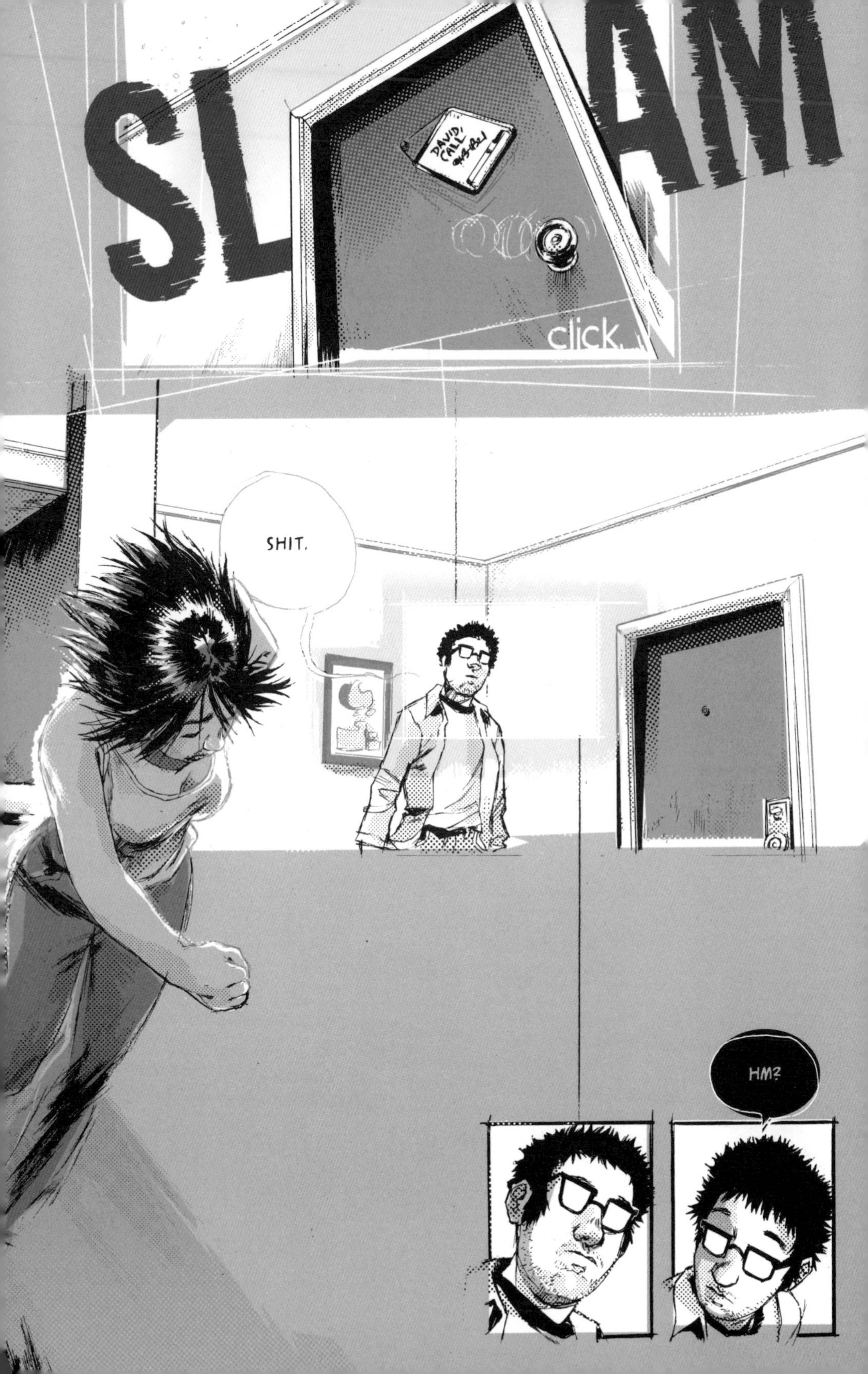
SLAM
DAVID, CALL
click.
SHIT.
HM?

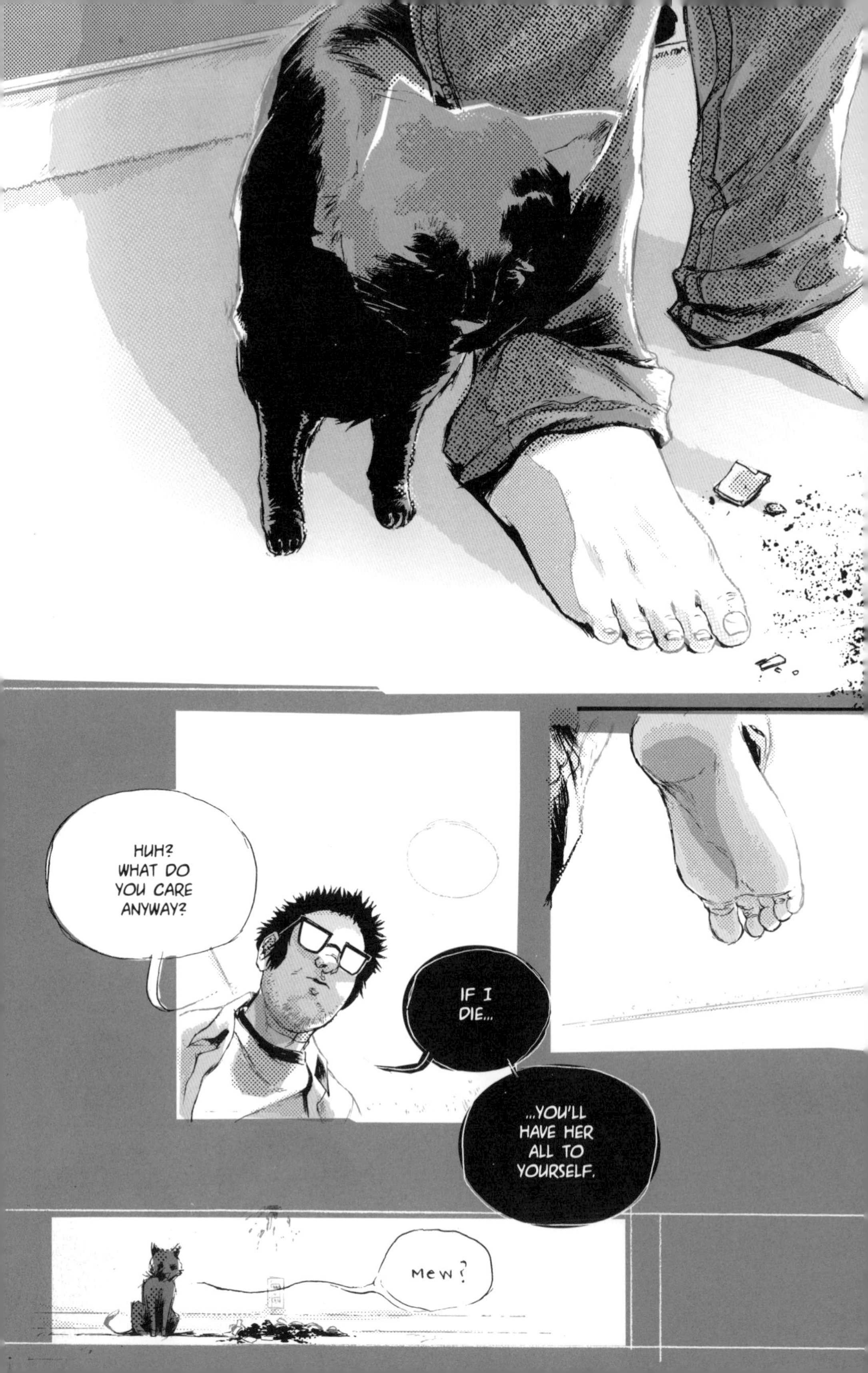
HUH? WHAT DO YOU CARE ANYWAY?
IF I DIE...
...YOU'LL HAVE HER ALL TO YOURSELF.
Mew?

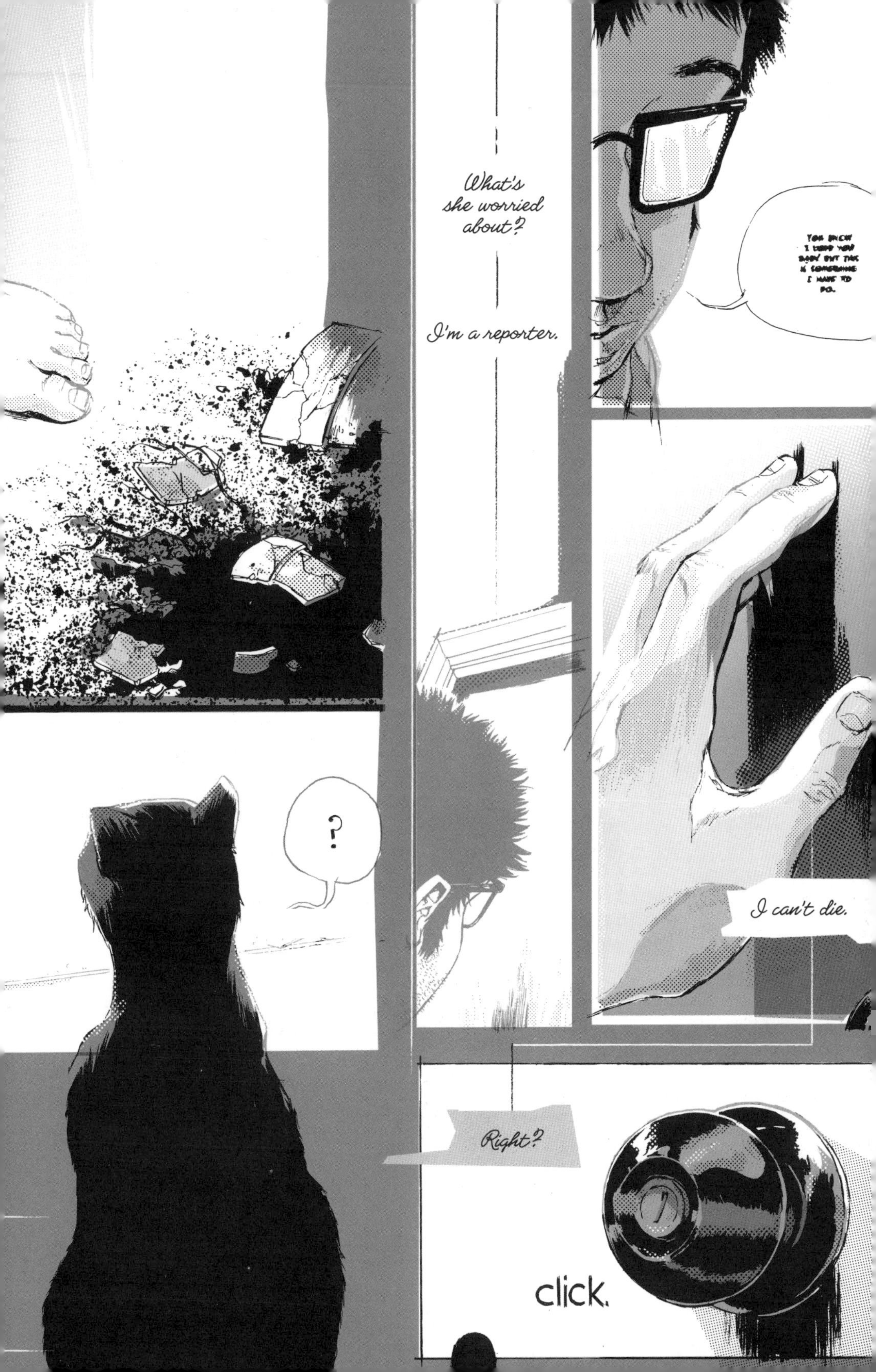
?
What's she worried about?
I'm a reporter.
I can't die.
Right?
click.

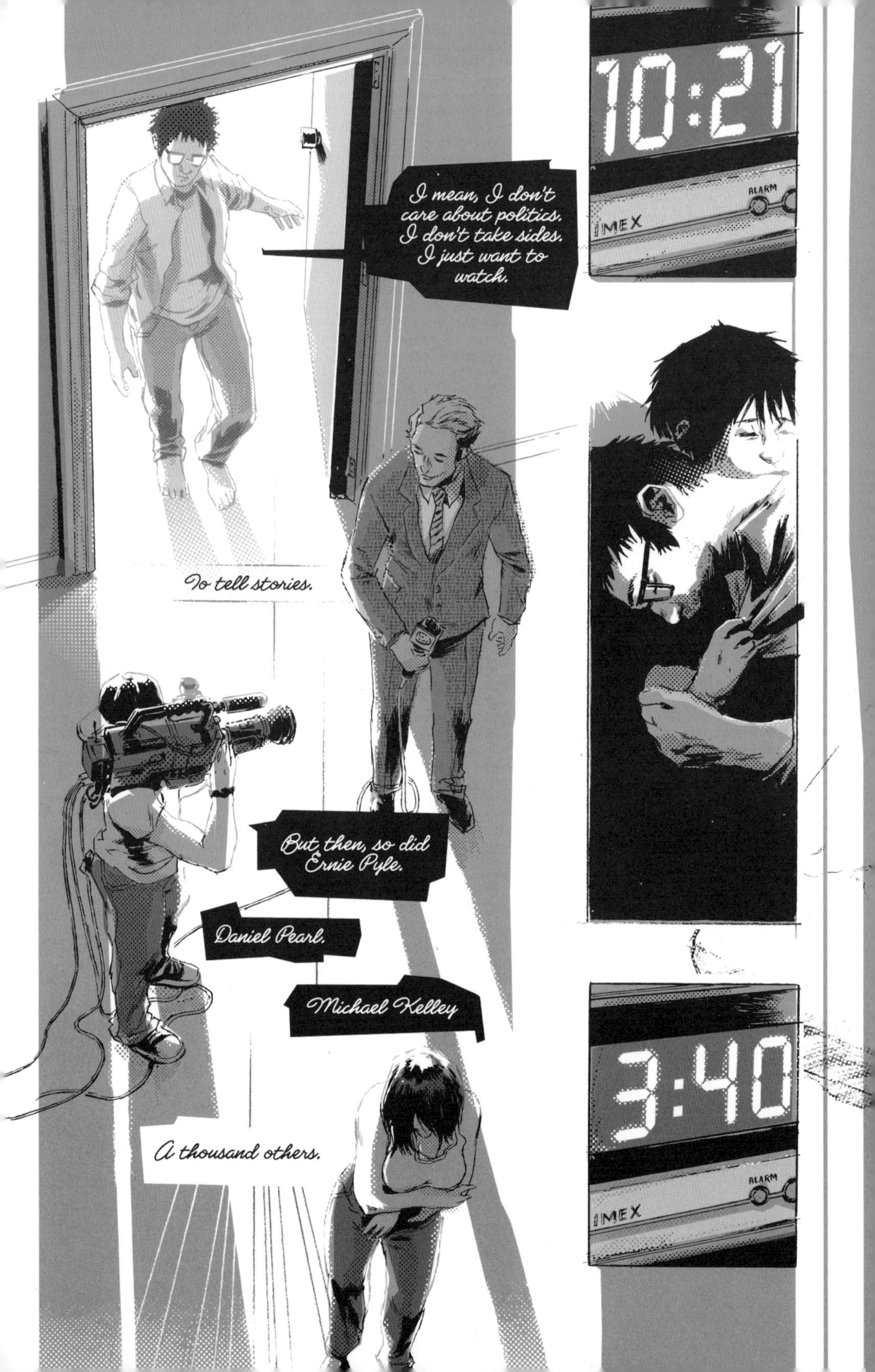

I mean, I don't care about politics. I don't take sides. I just want to watch.
10:21
ALARM
IMEX
To tell stories.
But then, so did Ernie Pyle.
Daniel Pearl.
Michael Kelley
A thousand others.
3:40
ALARM
IMEX

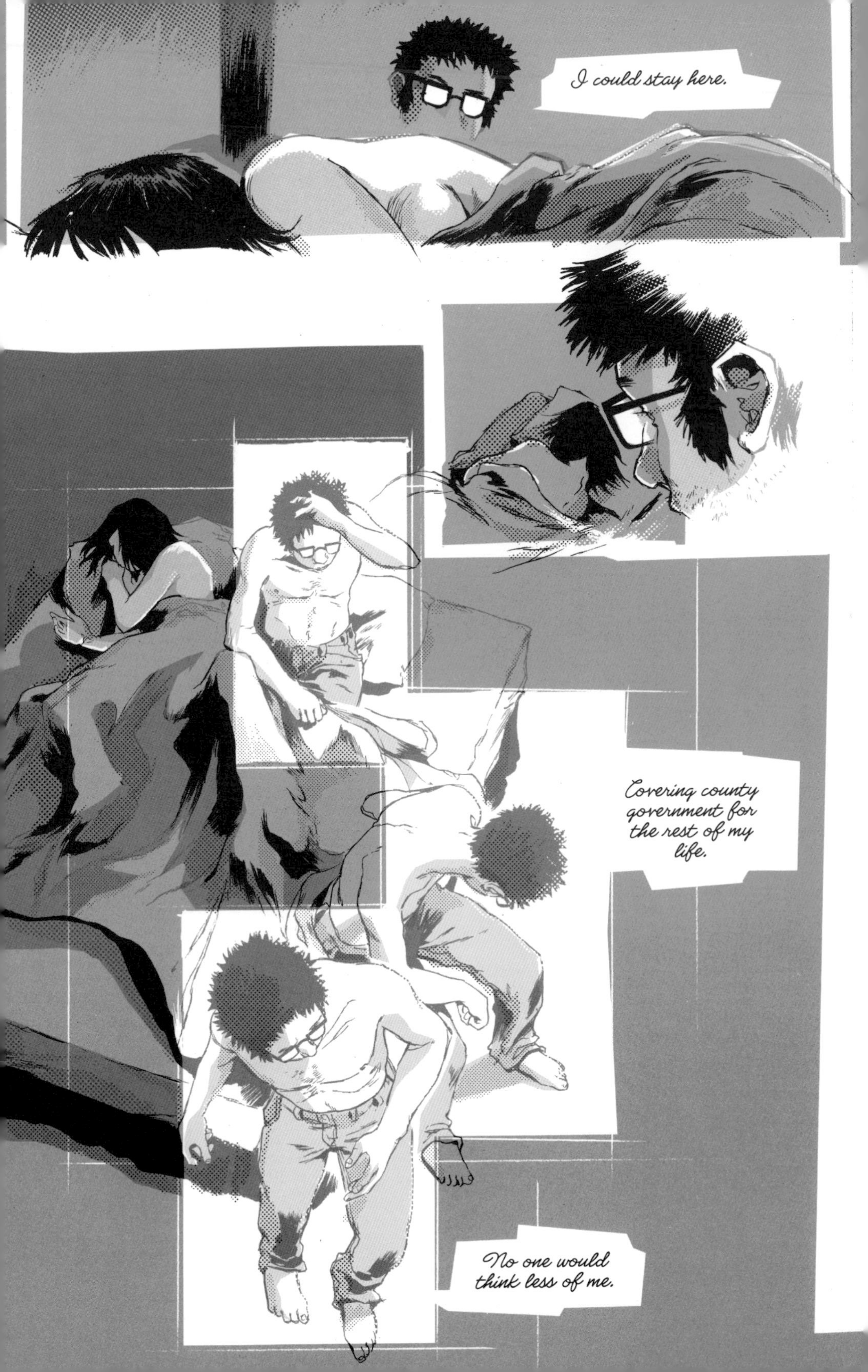
I could stay here.
Covering county government for the rest of my life.
No one would think less of me.

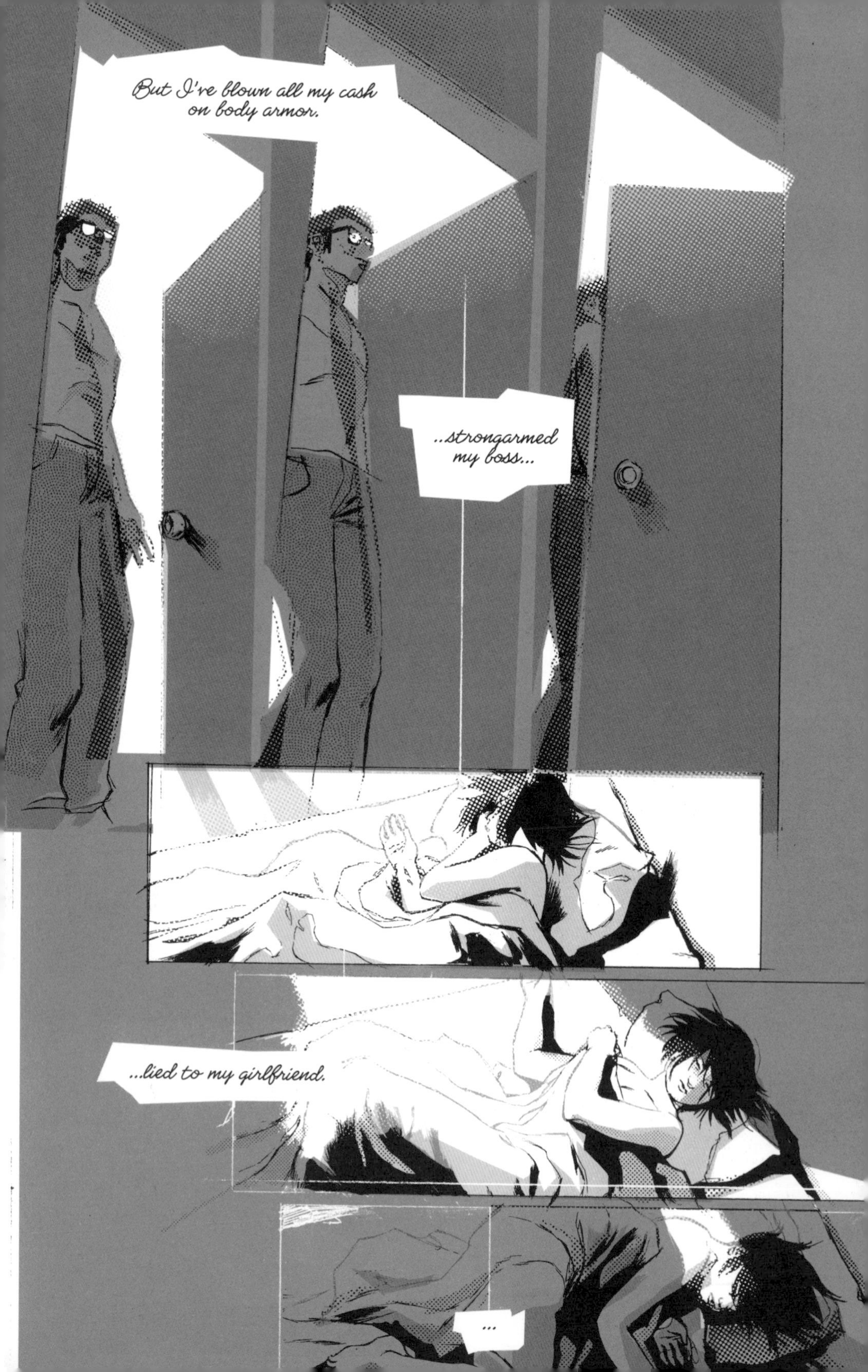
But I've blown all my cash on body armor.
...strongarmed my boss...
...lied to my girlfriend.
...

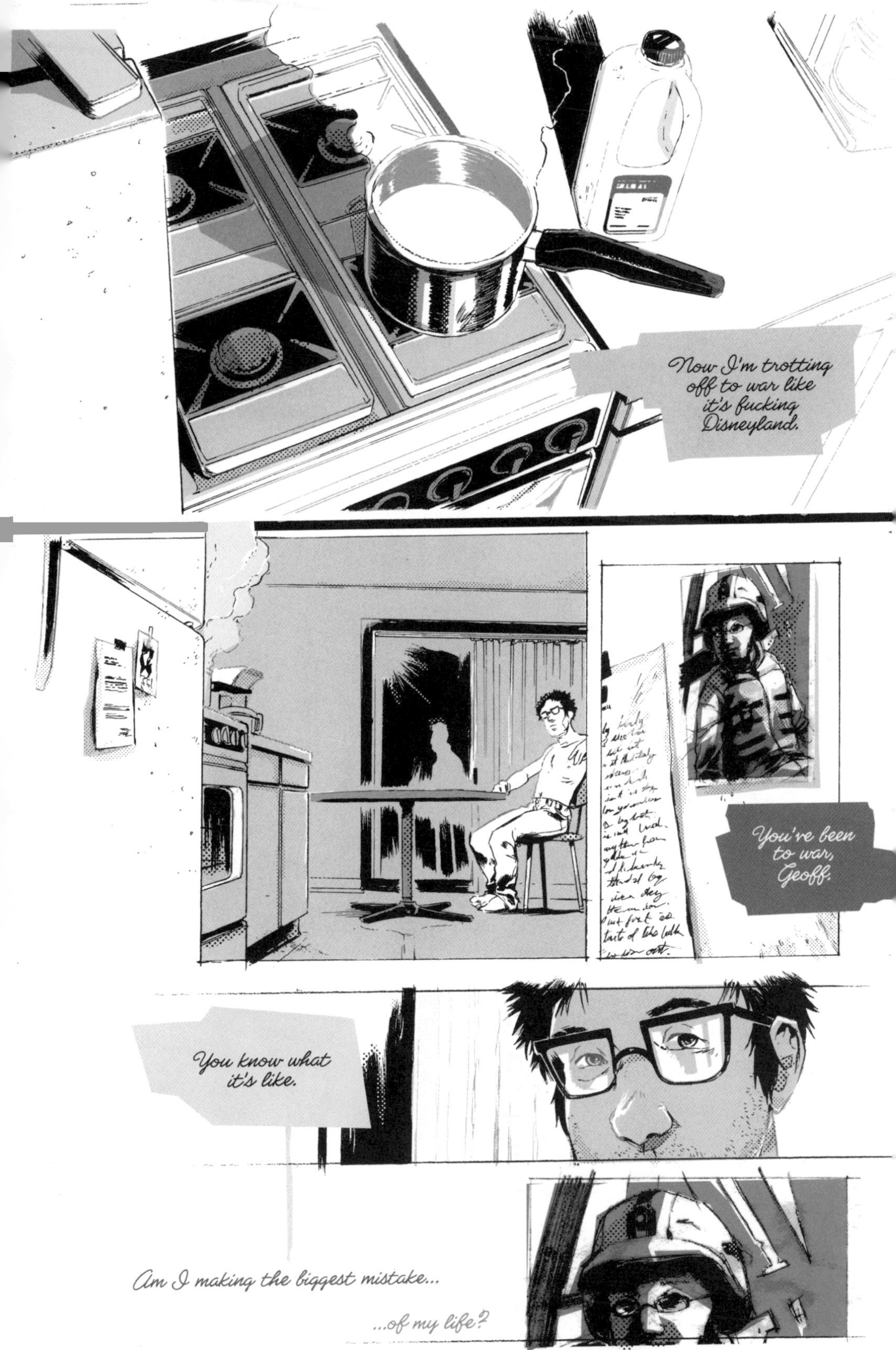
Now I'm trotting off to war like it's fucking Disneyland.
You've been to war, Geoff.
You know what it's like.
Am I making the biggest mistake...
...of my life?

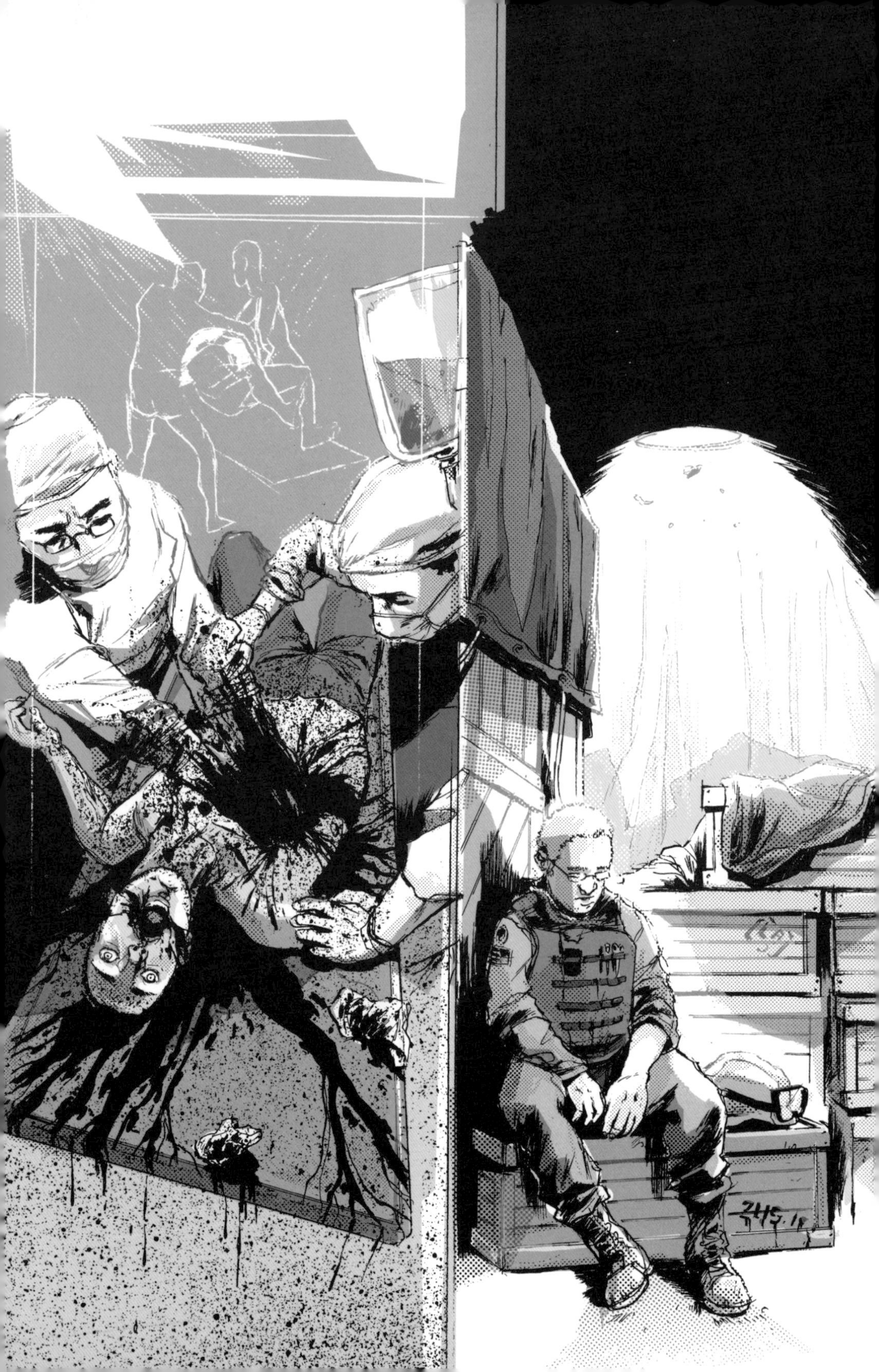

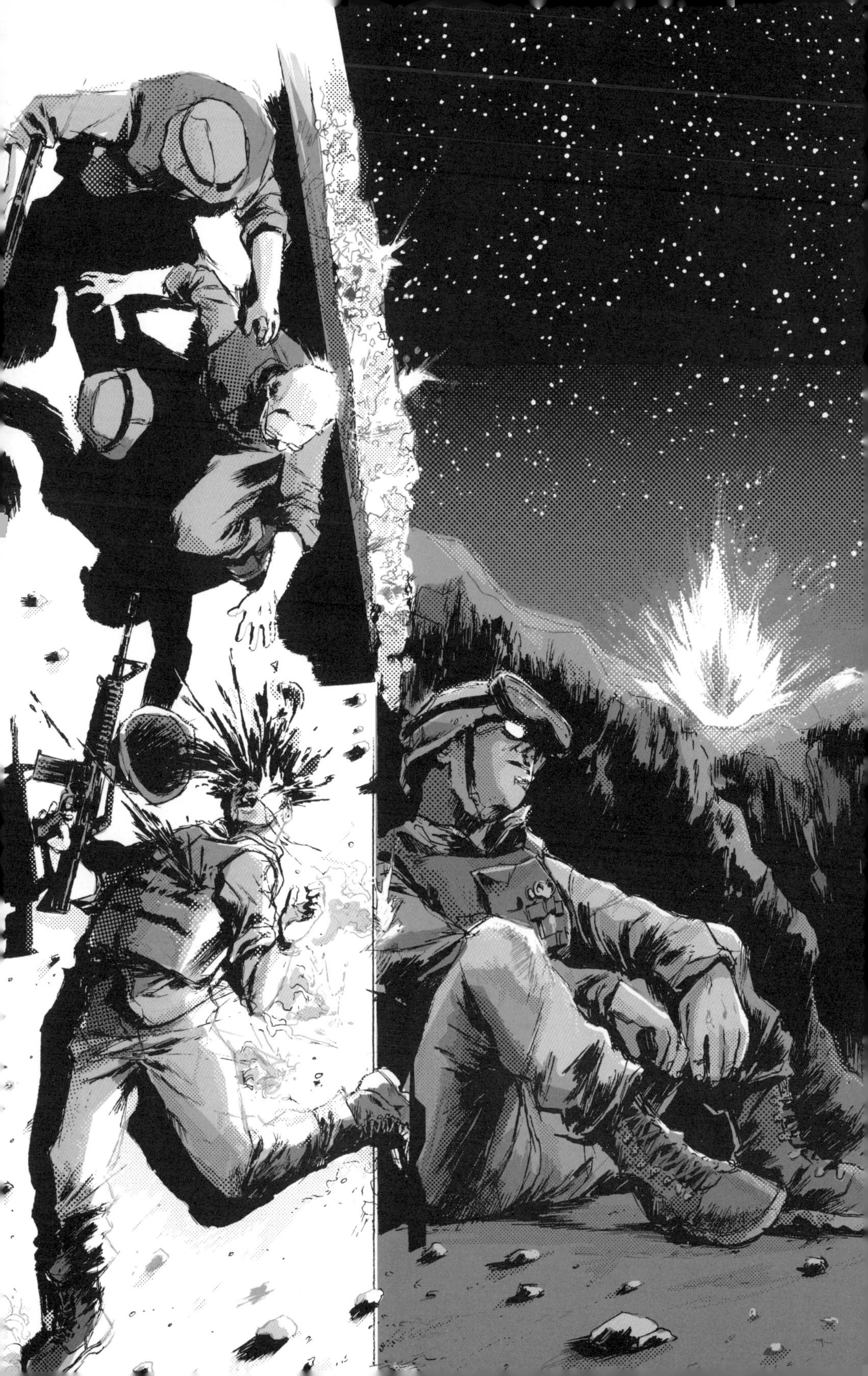

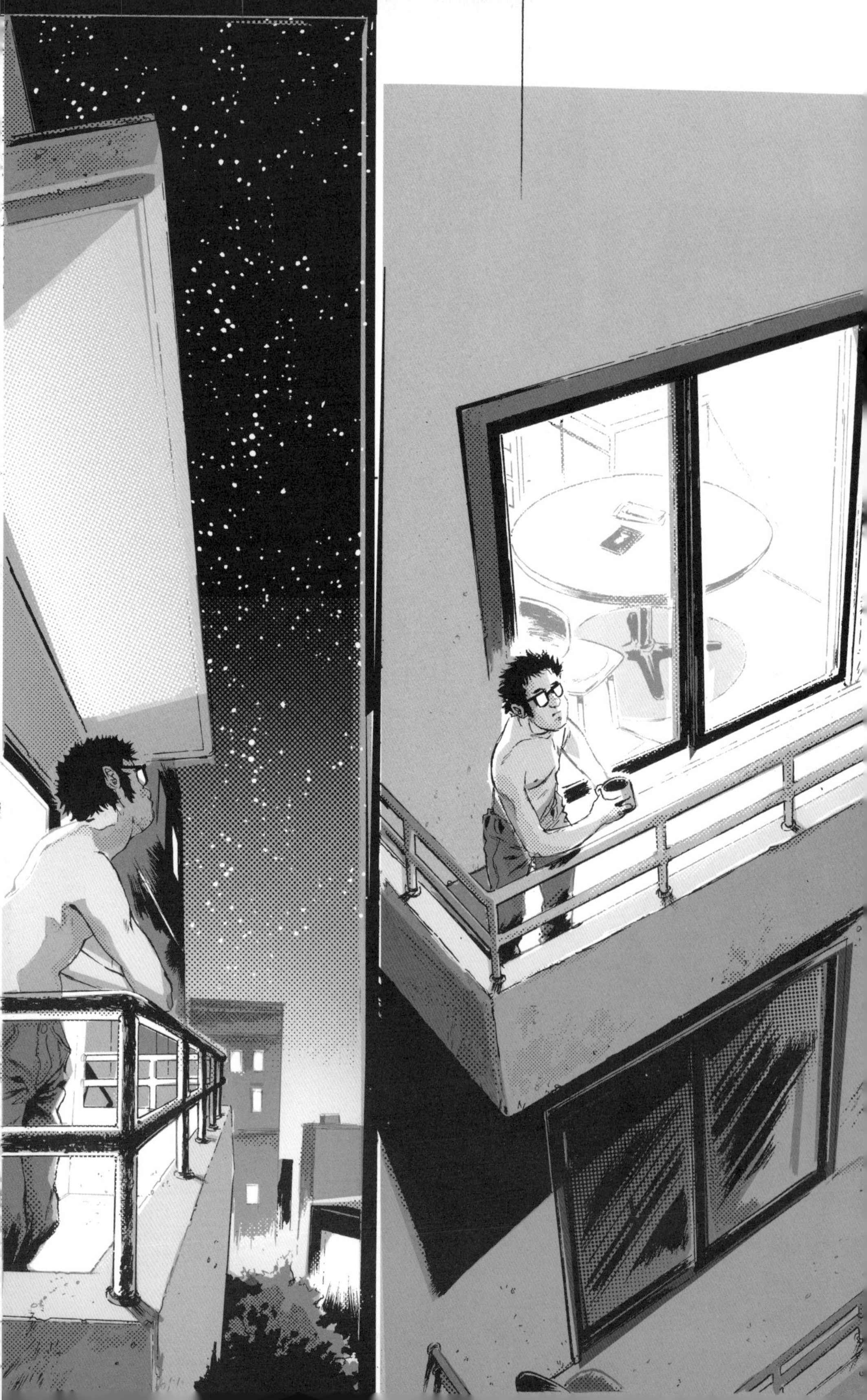

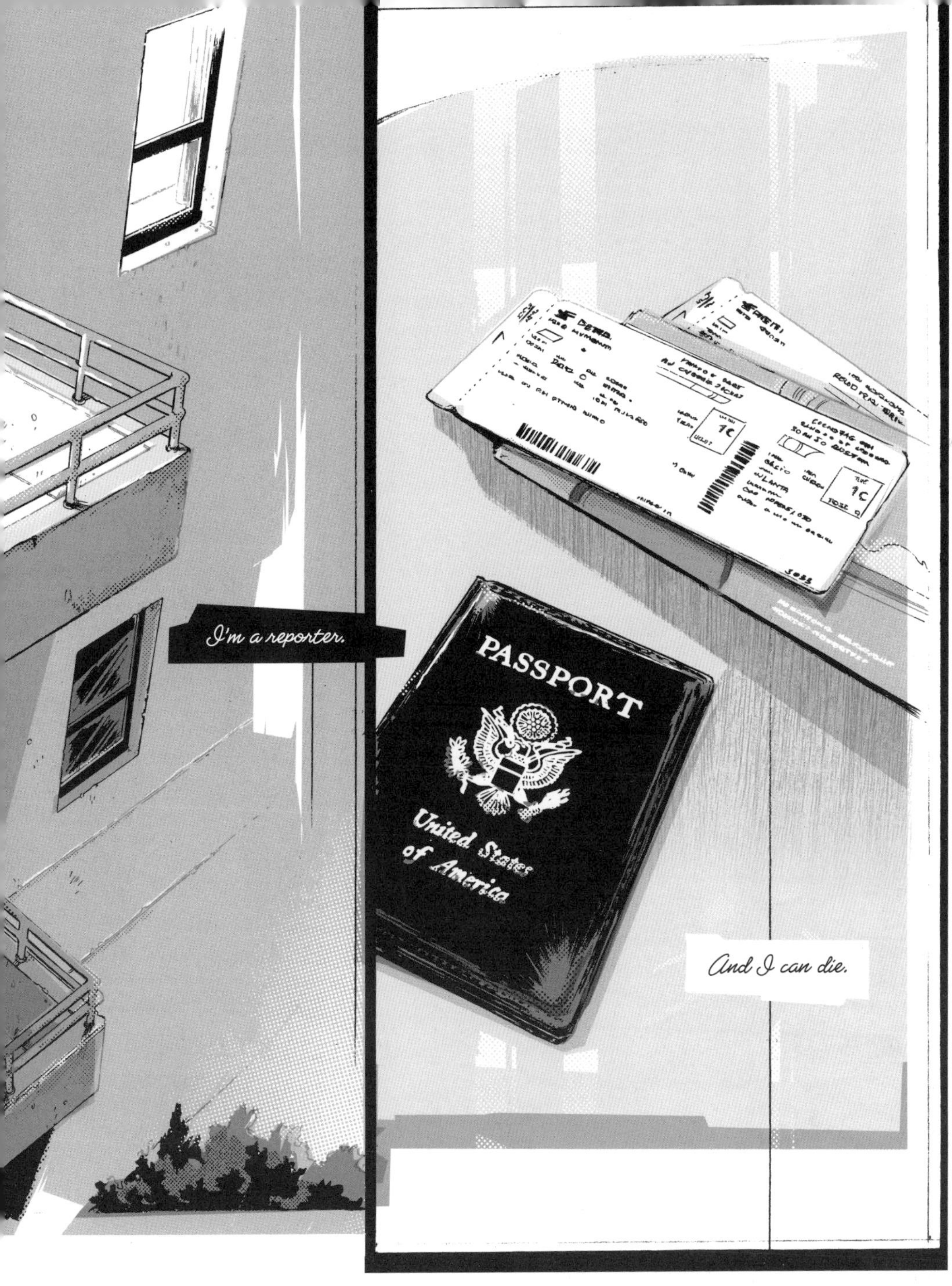
I'm a reporter.
And I can die.
PASSPORT
United States of America

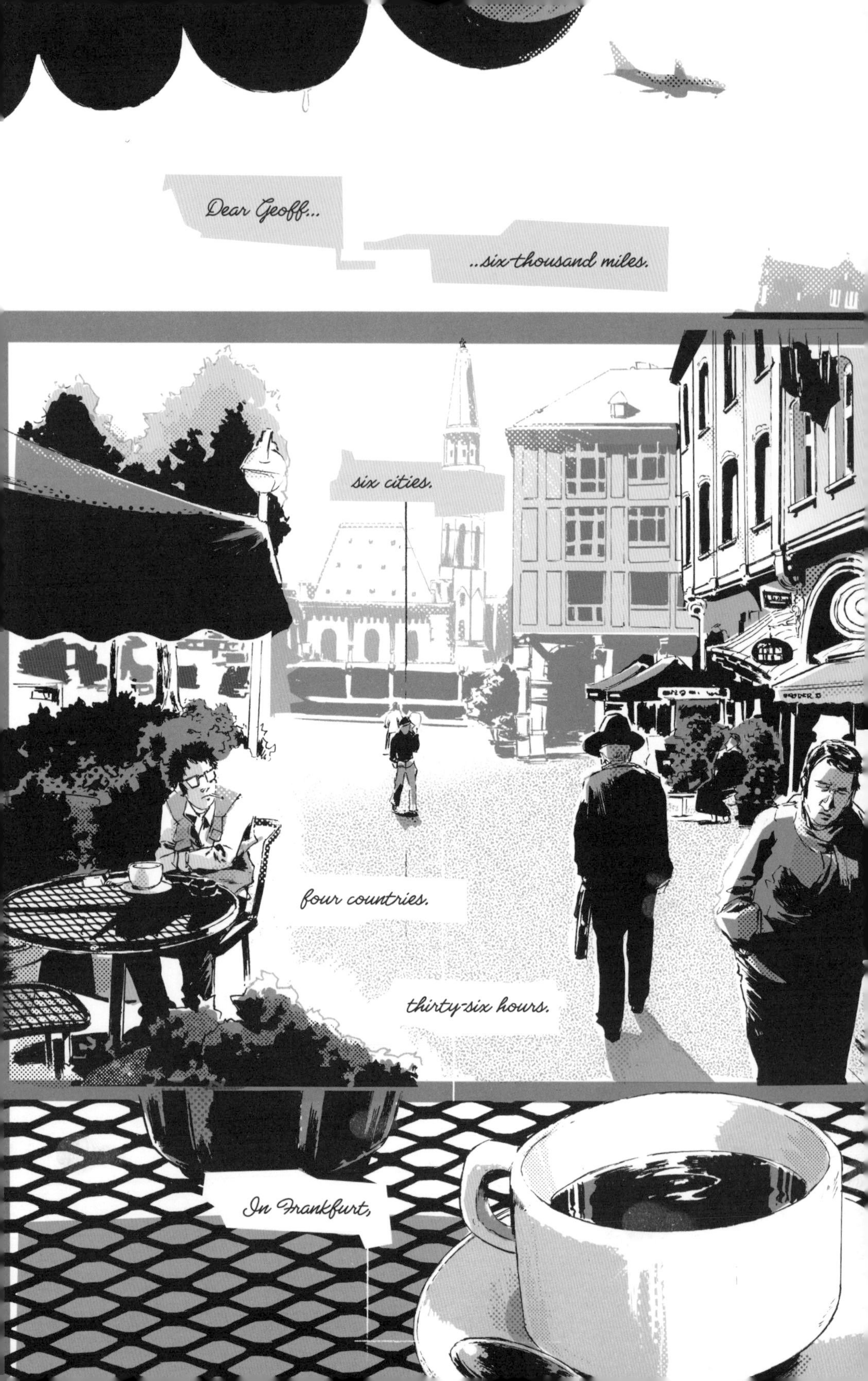
Dear Geoff...
..six thousand miles.
six cities.
four countries.
thirty-six hours.
In Frankfurt,

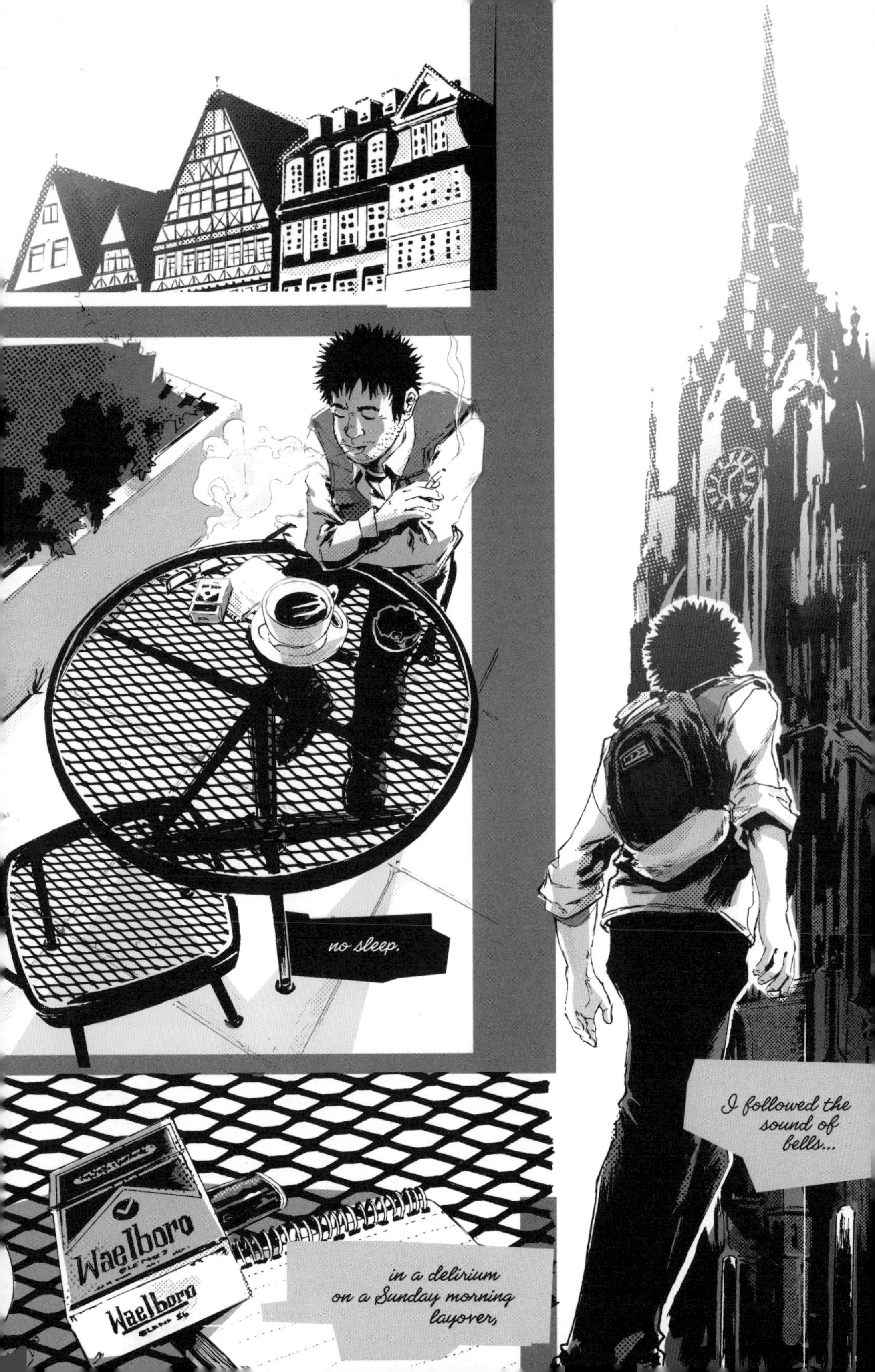
no sleep.
in a delirium on a Sunday morning layover,
I followed the sound of bells...
Waelboro
Waelboro

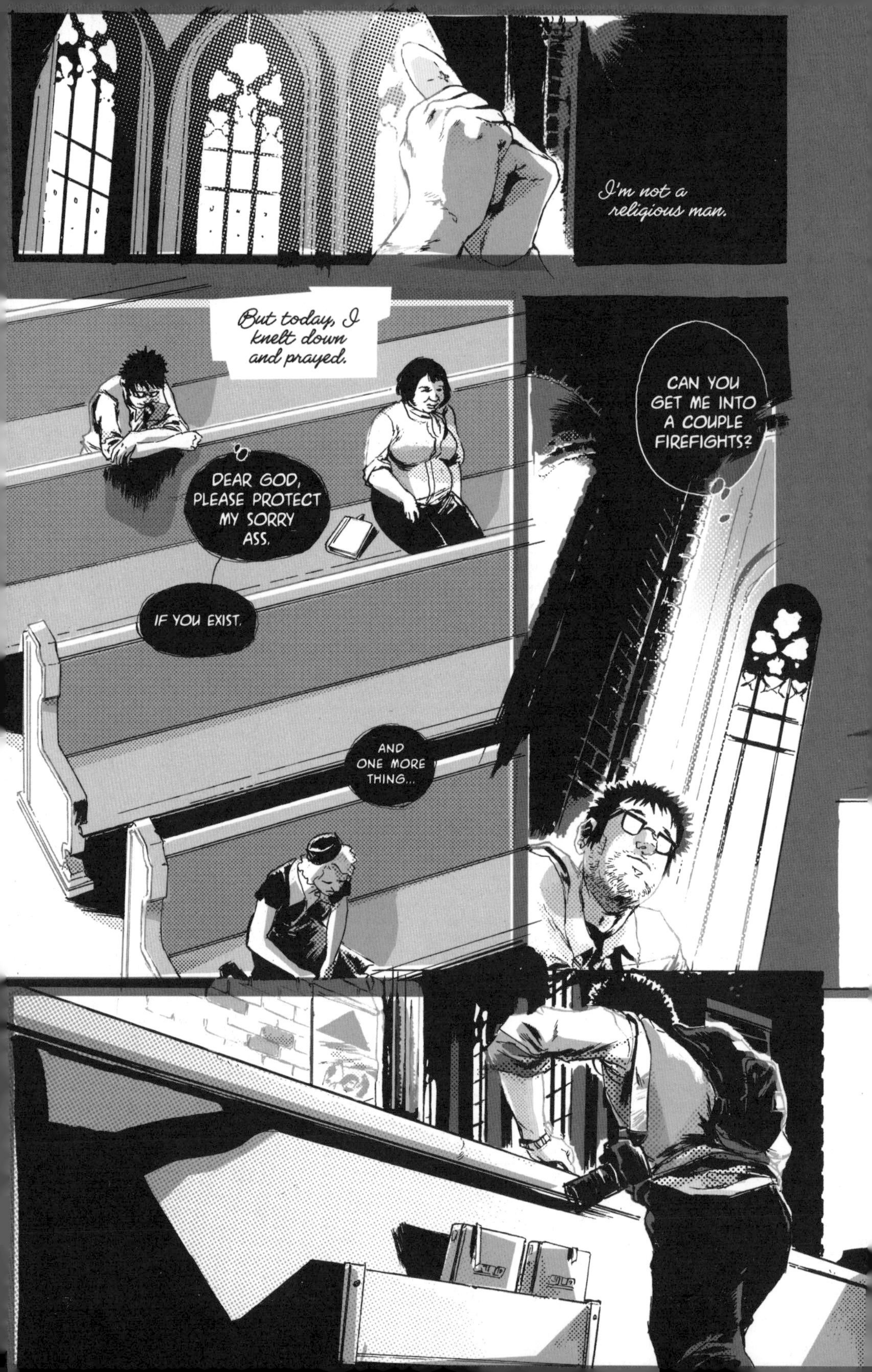
I'm not a religious man.
But today, I knelt down and prayed.
DEAR GOD, PLEASE PROTECT MY SORRY ASS.
IF YOU EXIST.
CAN YOU GET ME INTO A COUPLE FIREFIGHTS?
AND ONE MORE THING...

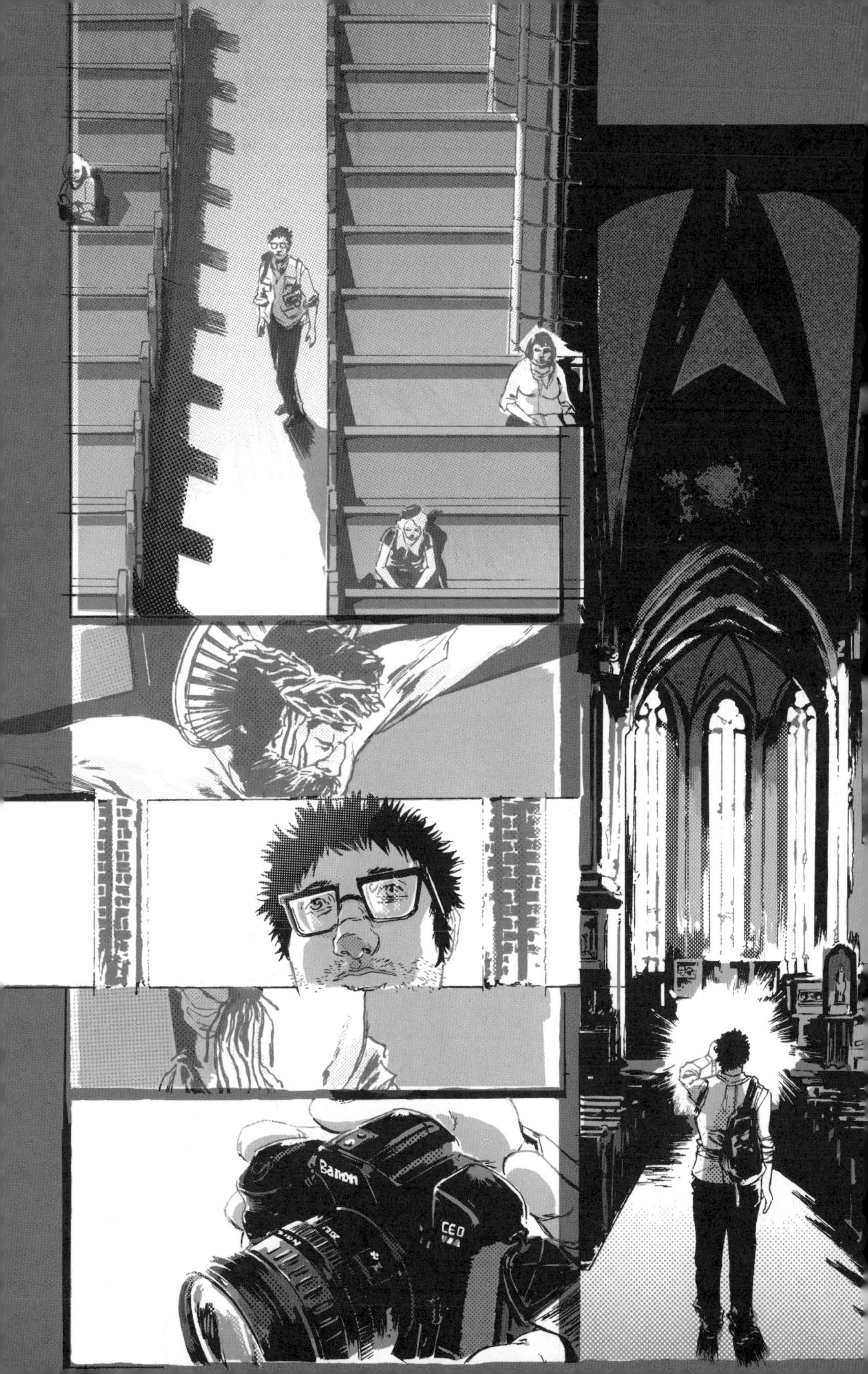
Banon
CEO

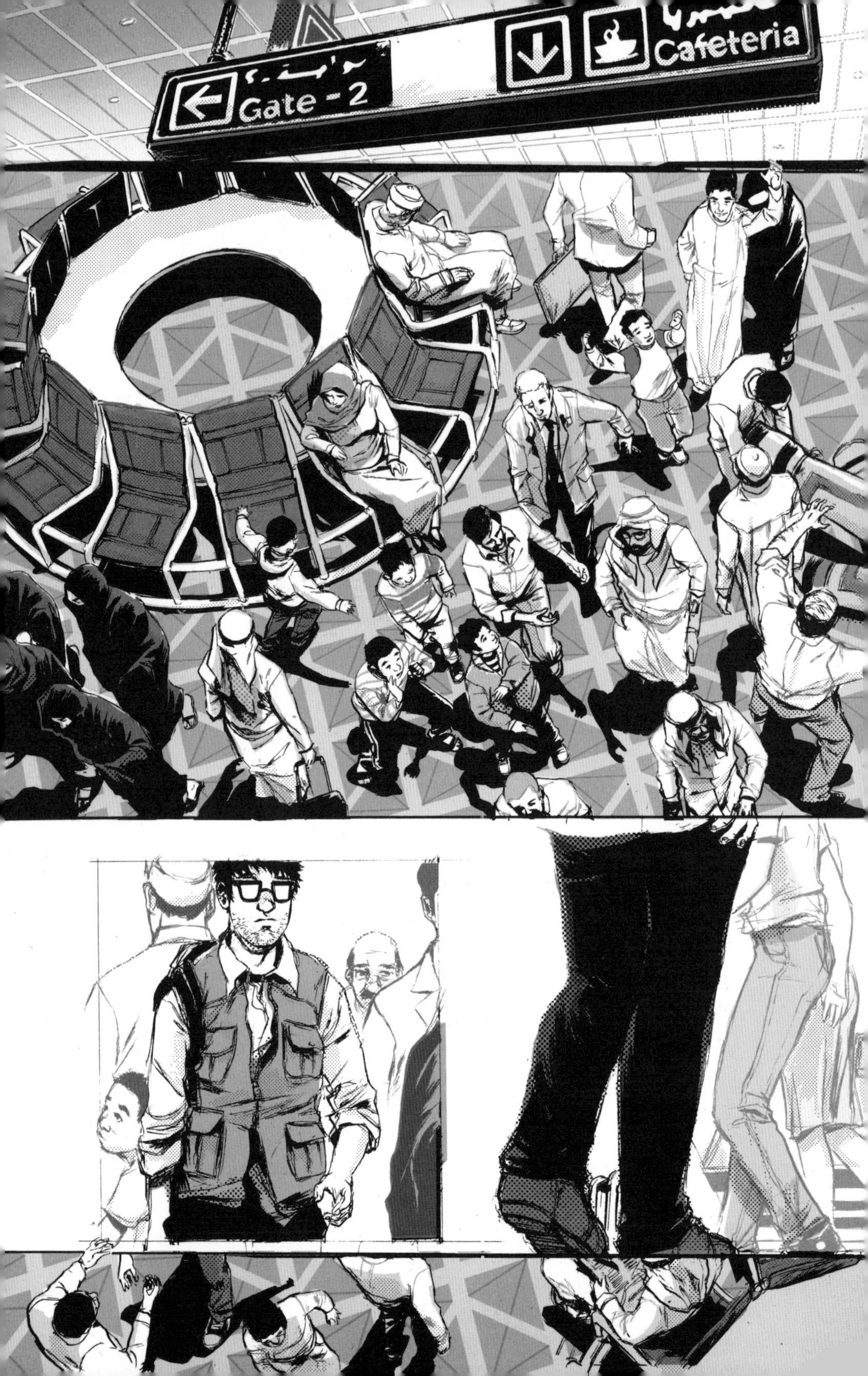
Gate - 2
Cafeteria

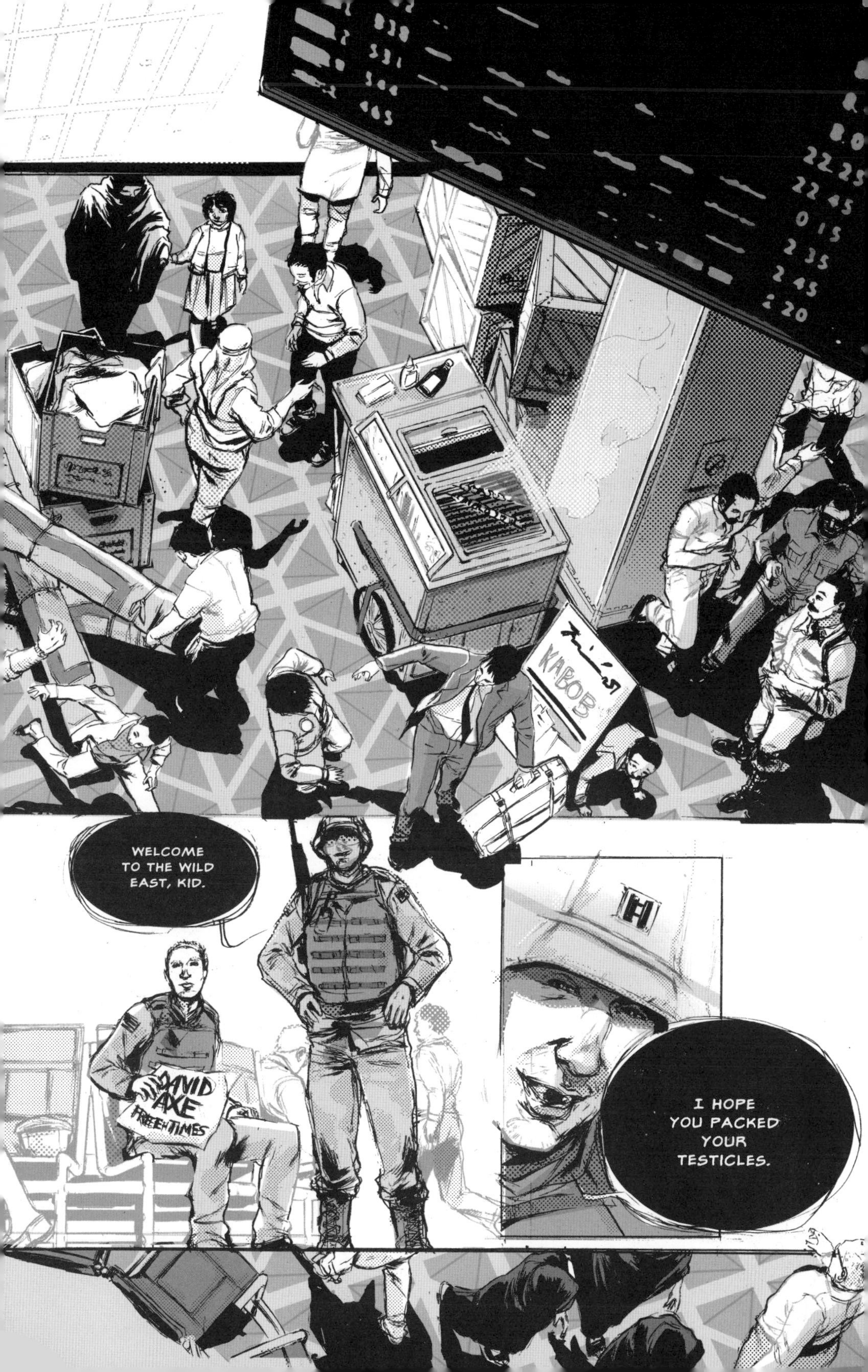
KABOB
WELCOME TO THE WILD EAST, KID.
DAVID AXE
FREE TIMES
I HOPE YOU PACKED YOUR TESTICLES.

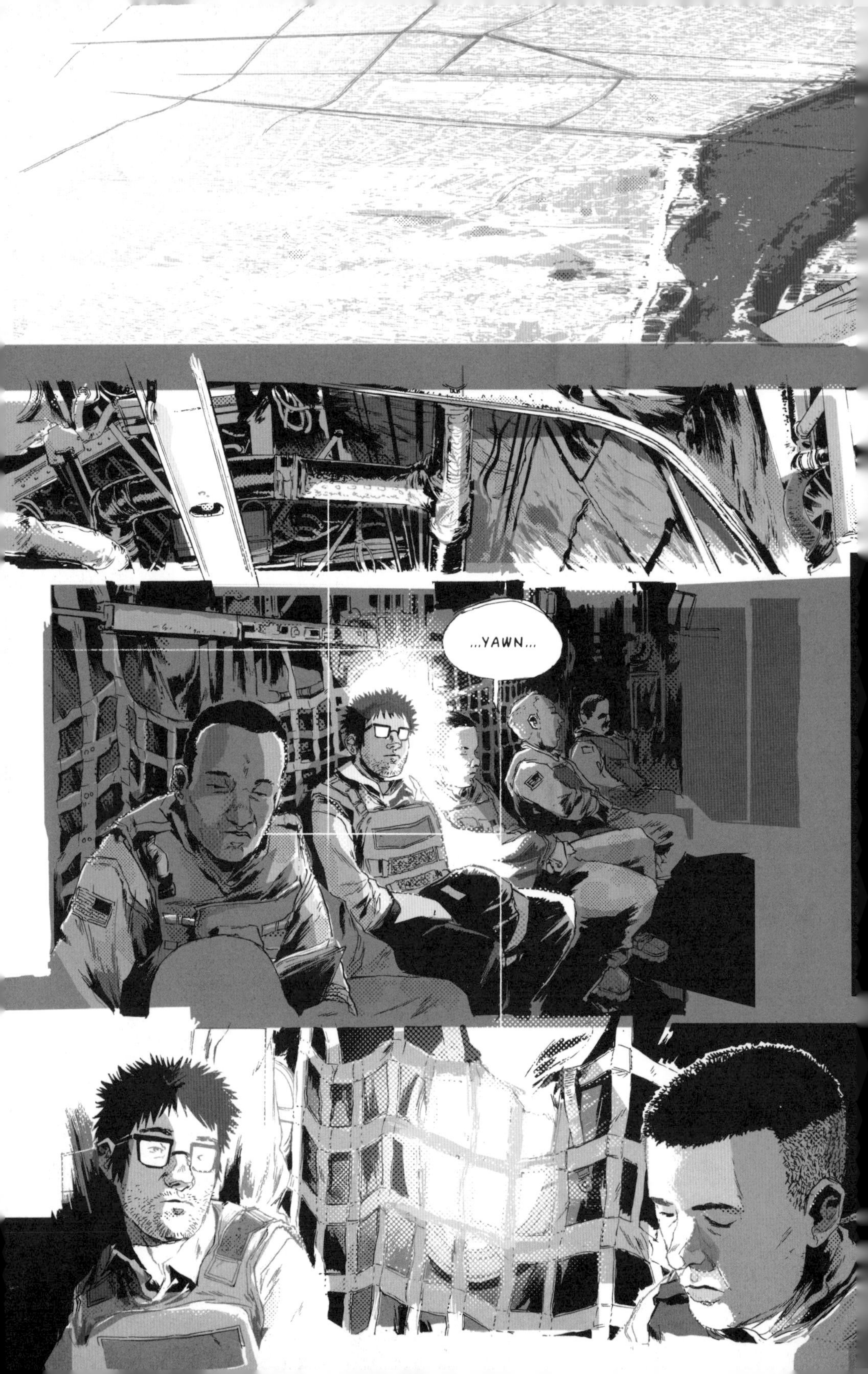
...YAWN...

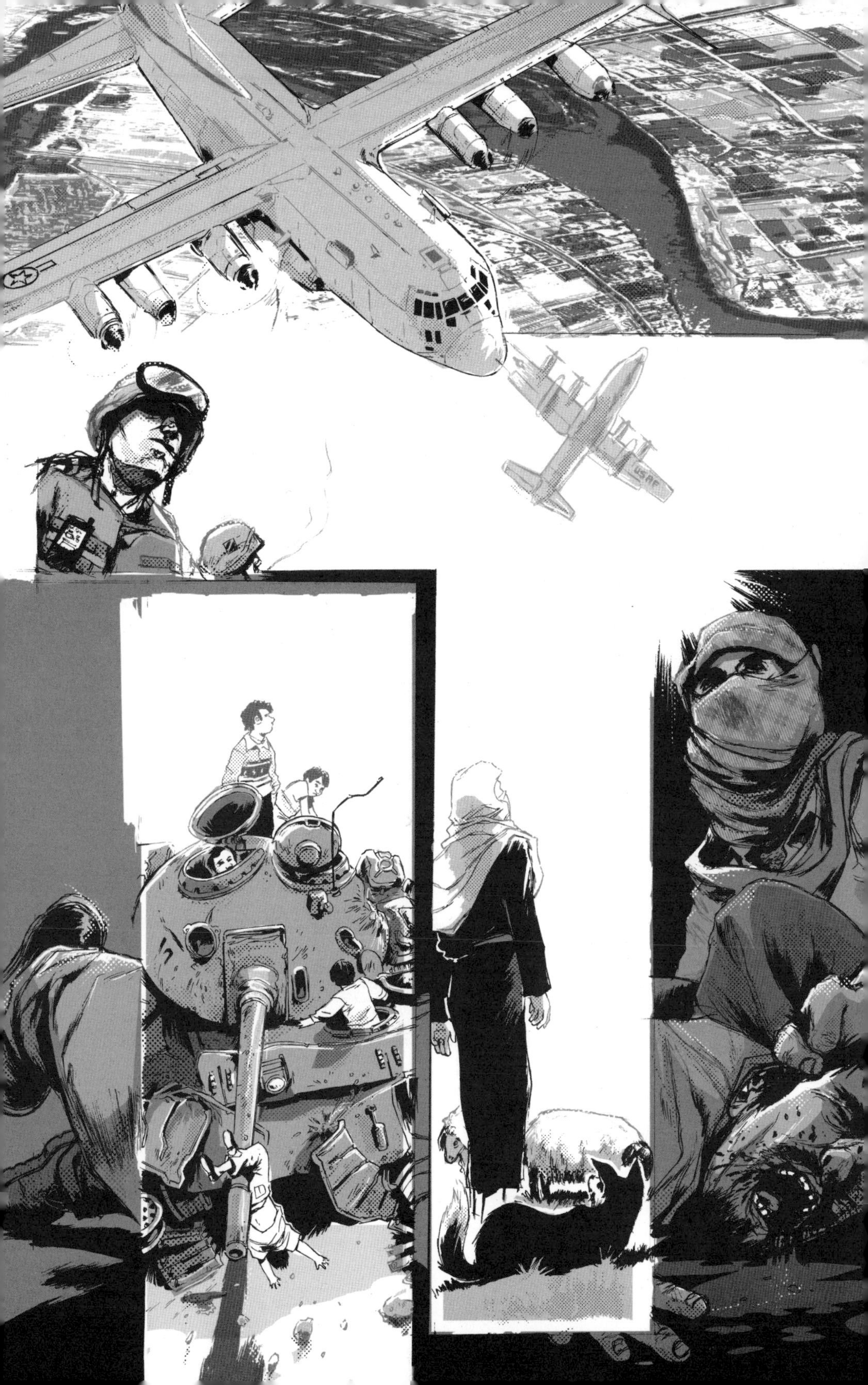
USAF

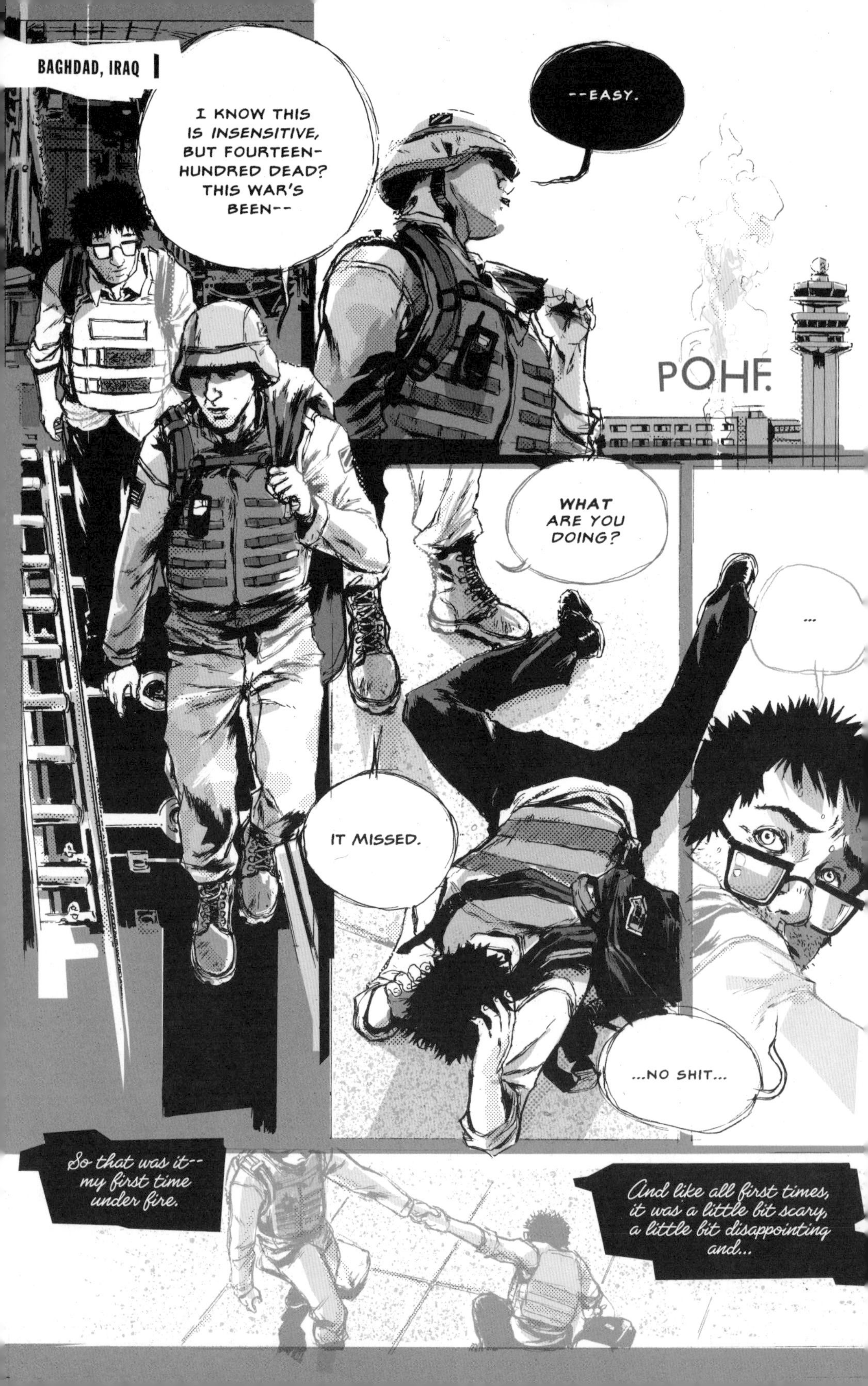
BAGHDAD, IRAQ
I KNOW THIS IS INSENSITIVE, BUT FOURTEEN-HUNDRED DEAD? THIS WAR'S BEEN--
--EASY.
POHF.
WHAT ARE YOU DOING?
IT MISSED.
...
...NO SHIT...
So that was it--my first time under fire.
And like all first times, it was a little bit scary, a little bit disappointing and...

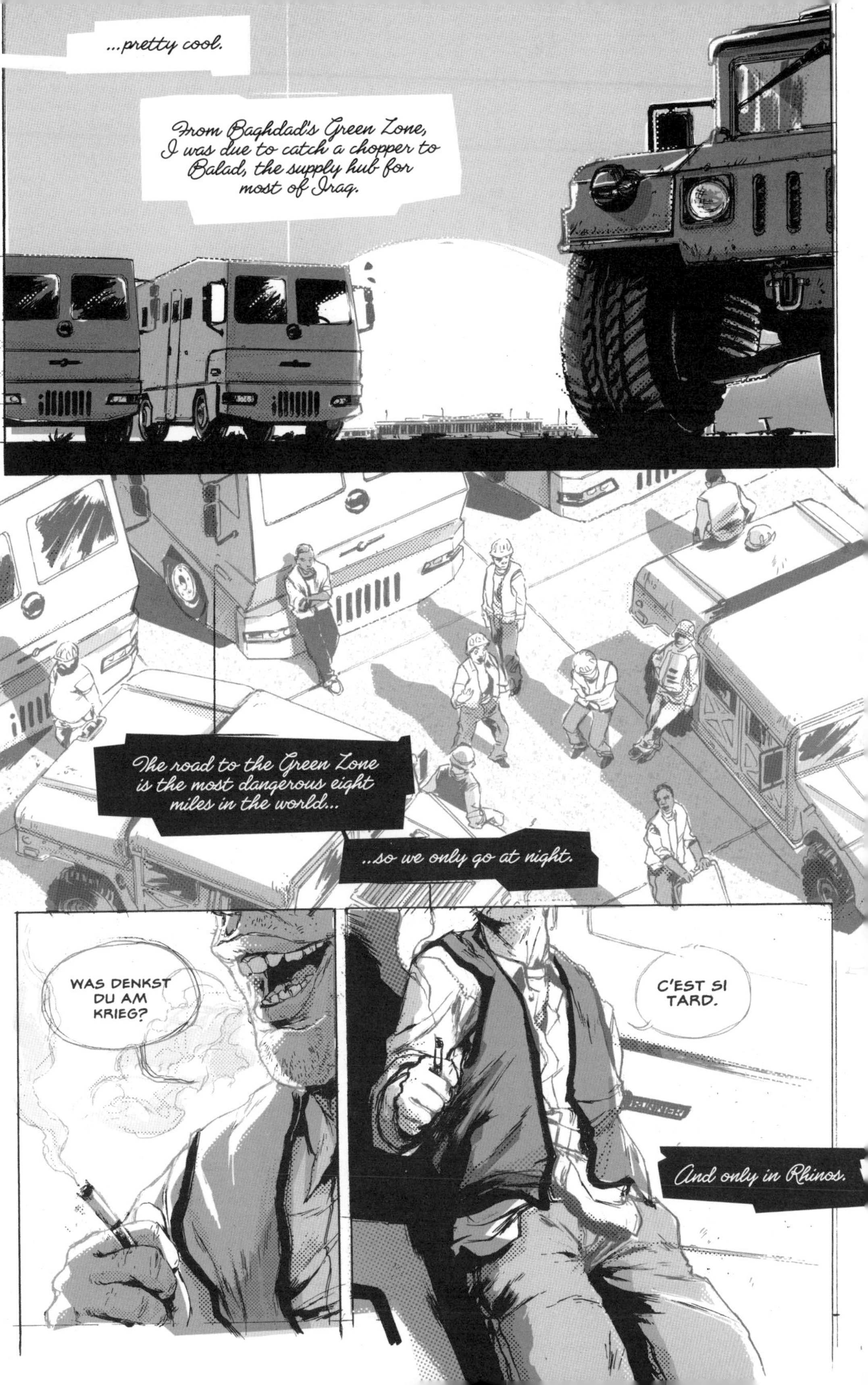
...pretty cool.
From Baghdad's Green Zone, I was due to catch a chopper to Balad, the supply hub for most of Iraq.
The road to the Green Zone is the most dangerous eight miles in the world...
...so we only go at night.
WAS DENKST DU AM KRIEG?
C'EST SI TARD.
And only in Rhinos.

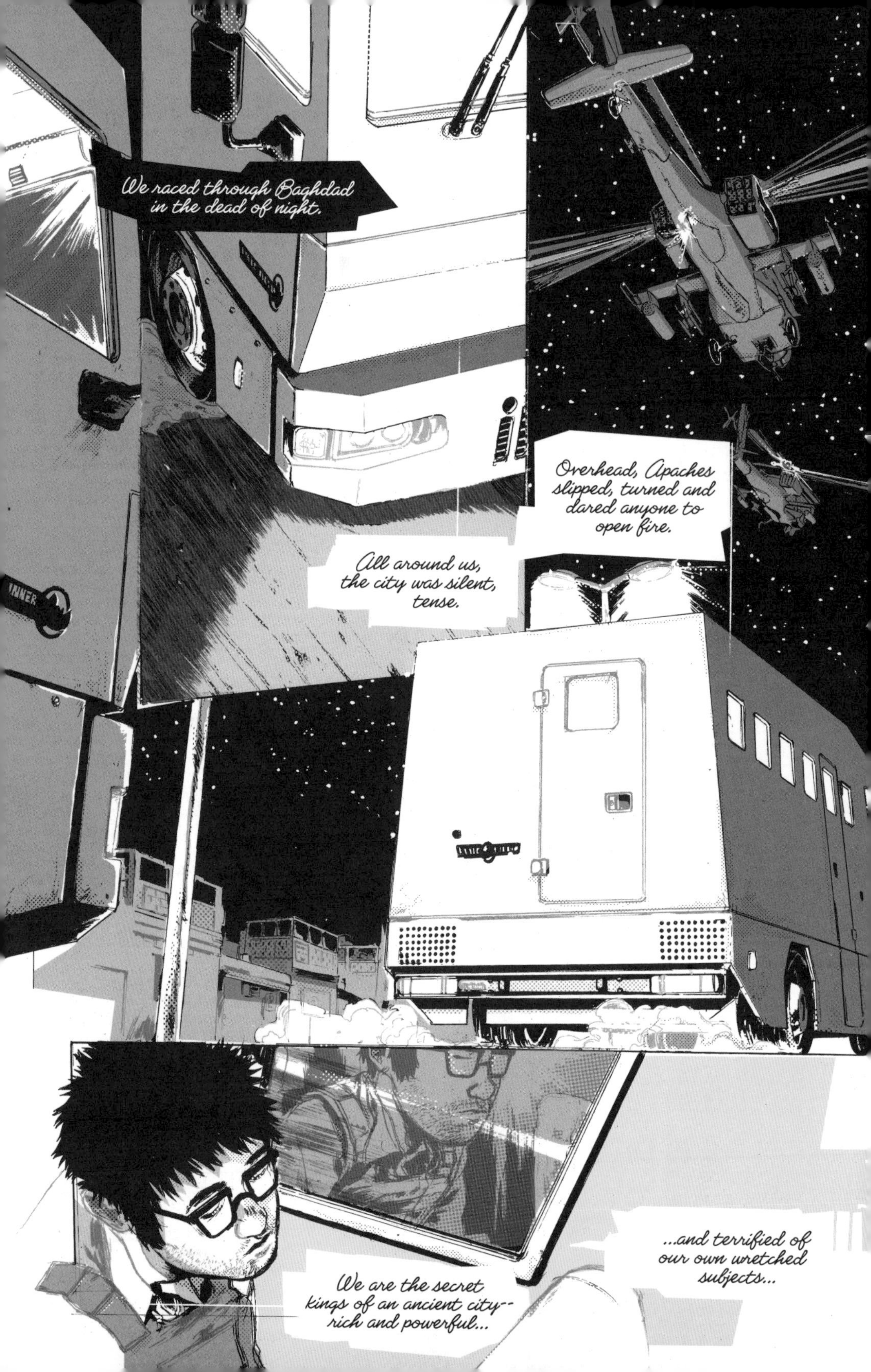
We raced through Baghdad in the dead of night.
Overhead, Apaches slipped, turned and dared anyone to open fire.
All around us, the city was silent, tense.
We are the secret kings of an ancient city-- rich and powerful...
...and terrified of our own wretched subjects...

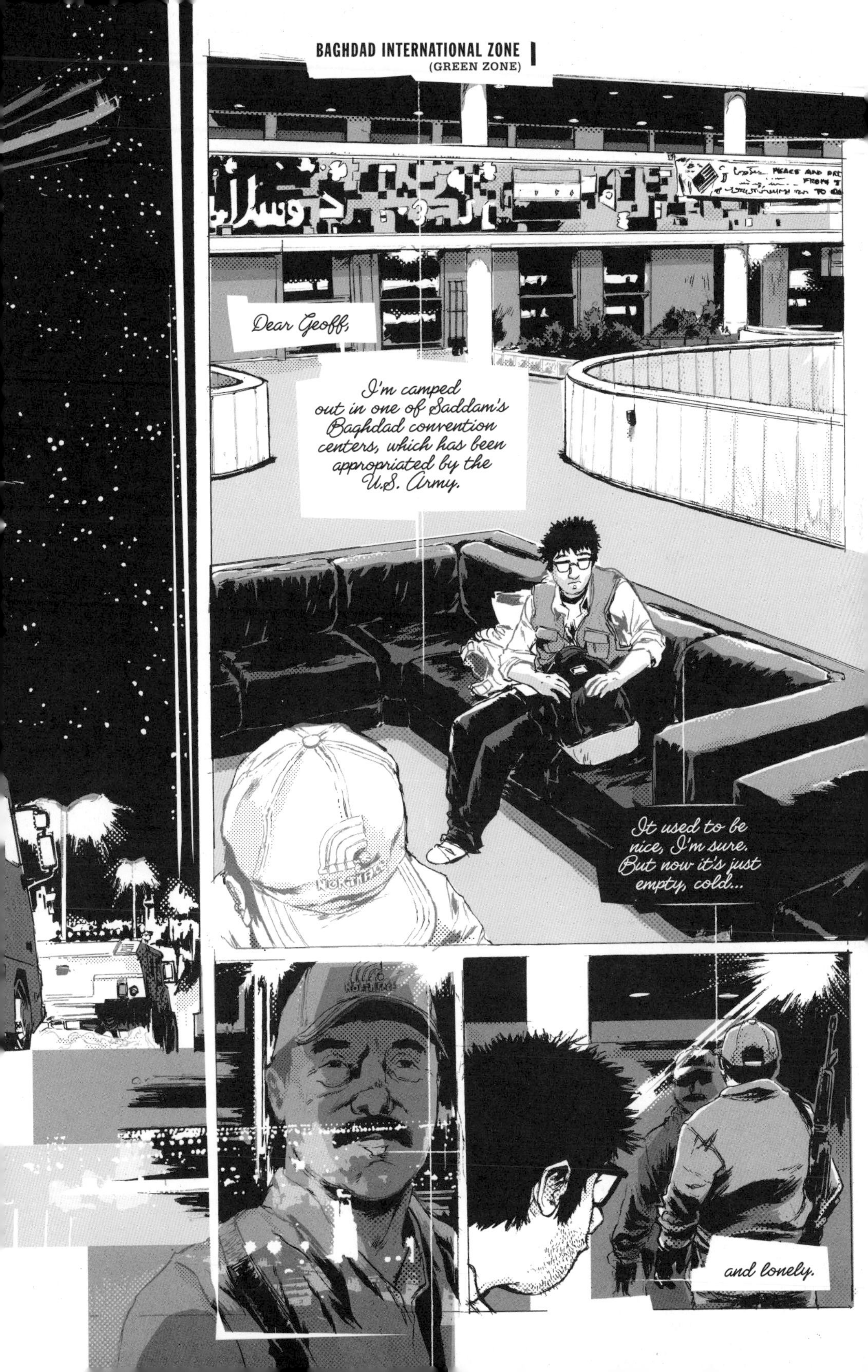
BAGHDAD INTERNATIONAL ZONE
(GREEN ZONE)
Dear Geoff,
I'm camped out in one of Saddam's Baghdad convention centers, which has been appropriated by the U.S. Army.
It used to be nice, I'm sure. But now it's just empty, cold...
and lonely.

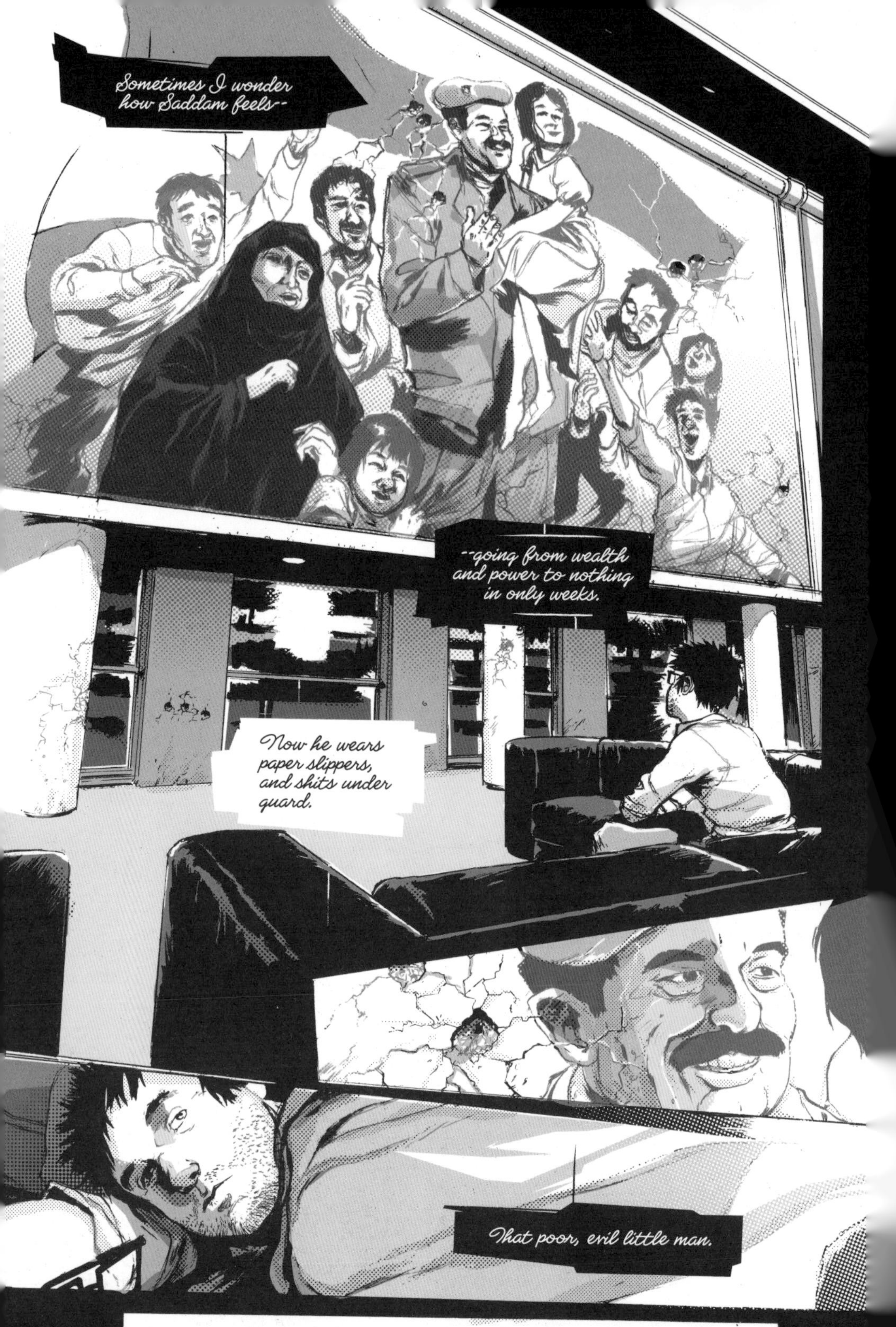
Sometimes I wonder how Saddam feels--
--going from wealth and power to nothing in only weeks.
Now he wears paper slippers, and shits under guard.
That poor, evil little man.

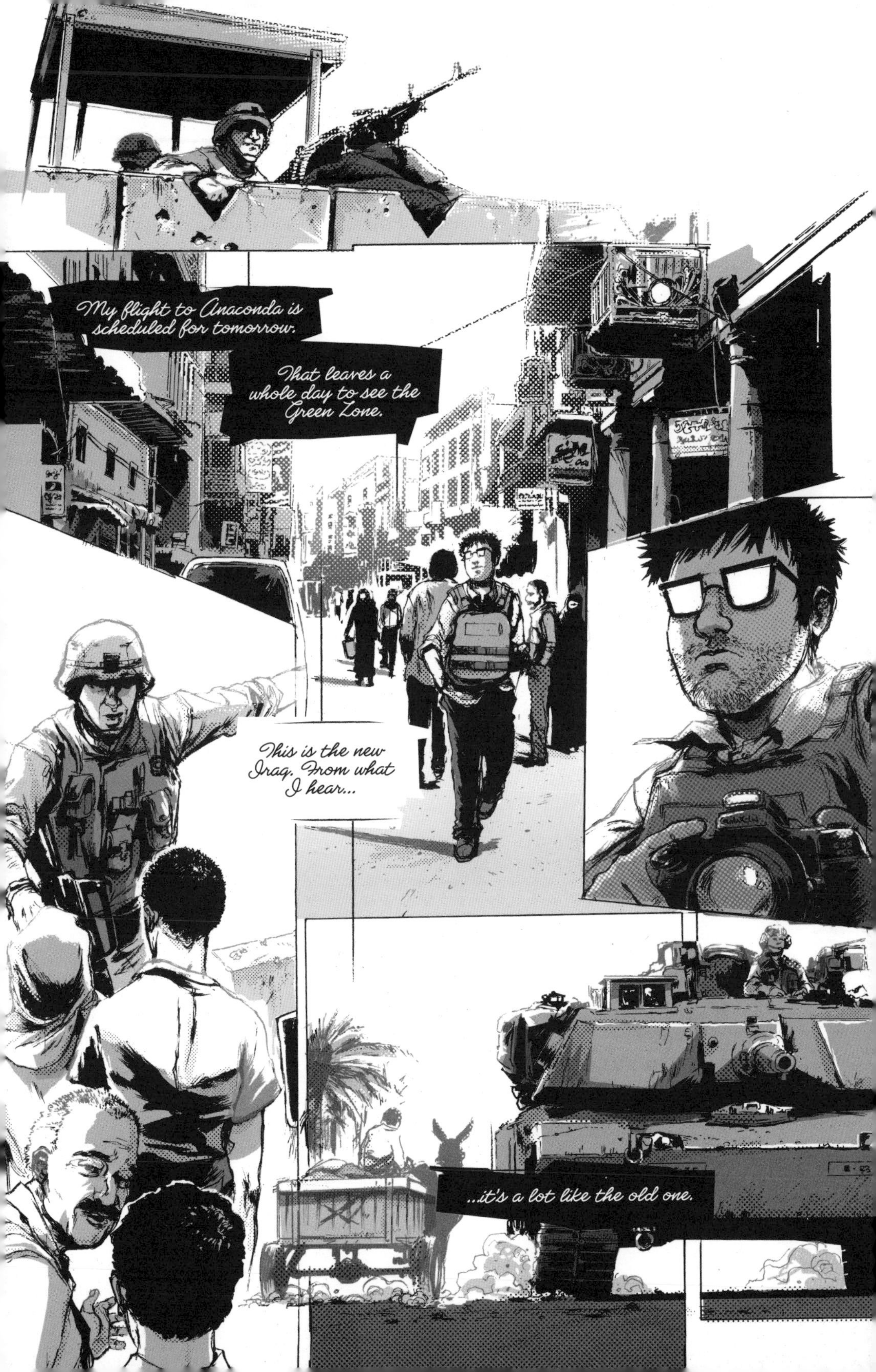
My flight to Anaconda is scheduled for tomorrow.
That leaves a whole day to see the Green Zone.
This is the new Iraq. From what I hear...
...it's a lot like the old one.

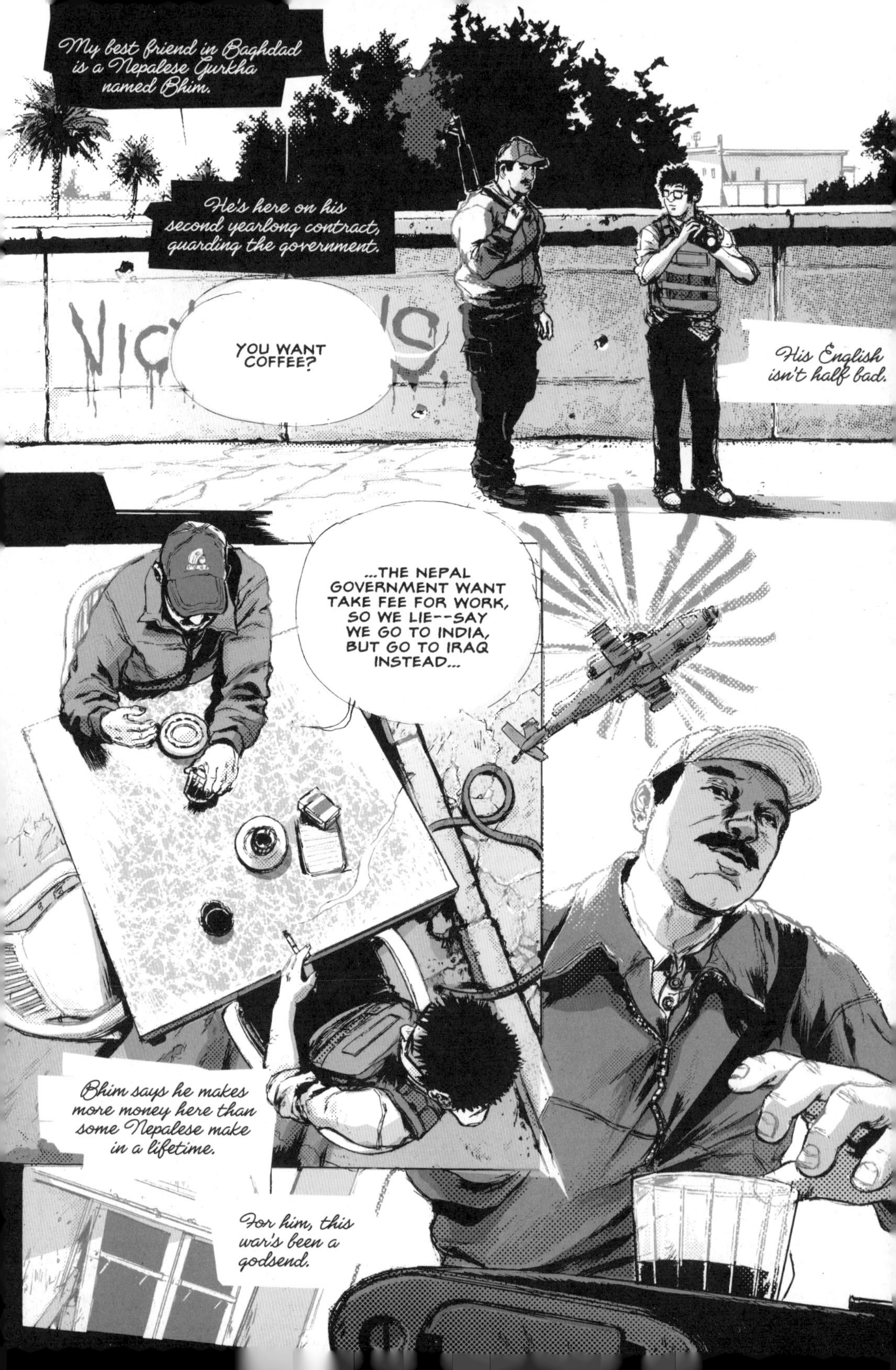
My best friend in Baghdad is a Nepalese Gurkha named Bhim.
He's here on his second yearlong contract, guarding the government.
YOU WANT COFFEE?
His English isn't half bad.
...THE NEPAL GOVERNMENT WANT TAKE FEE FOR WORK, SO WE LIE--SAY WE GO TO INDIA, BUT GO TO IRAQ INSTEAD...
Bhim says he makes more money here than some Nepalese make in a lifetime.
For him, this war's been a godsend.

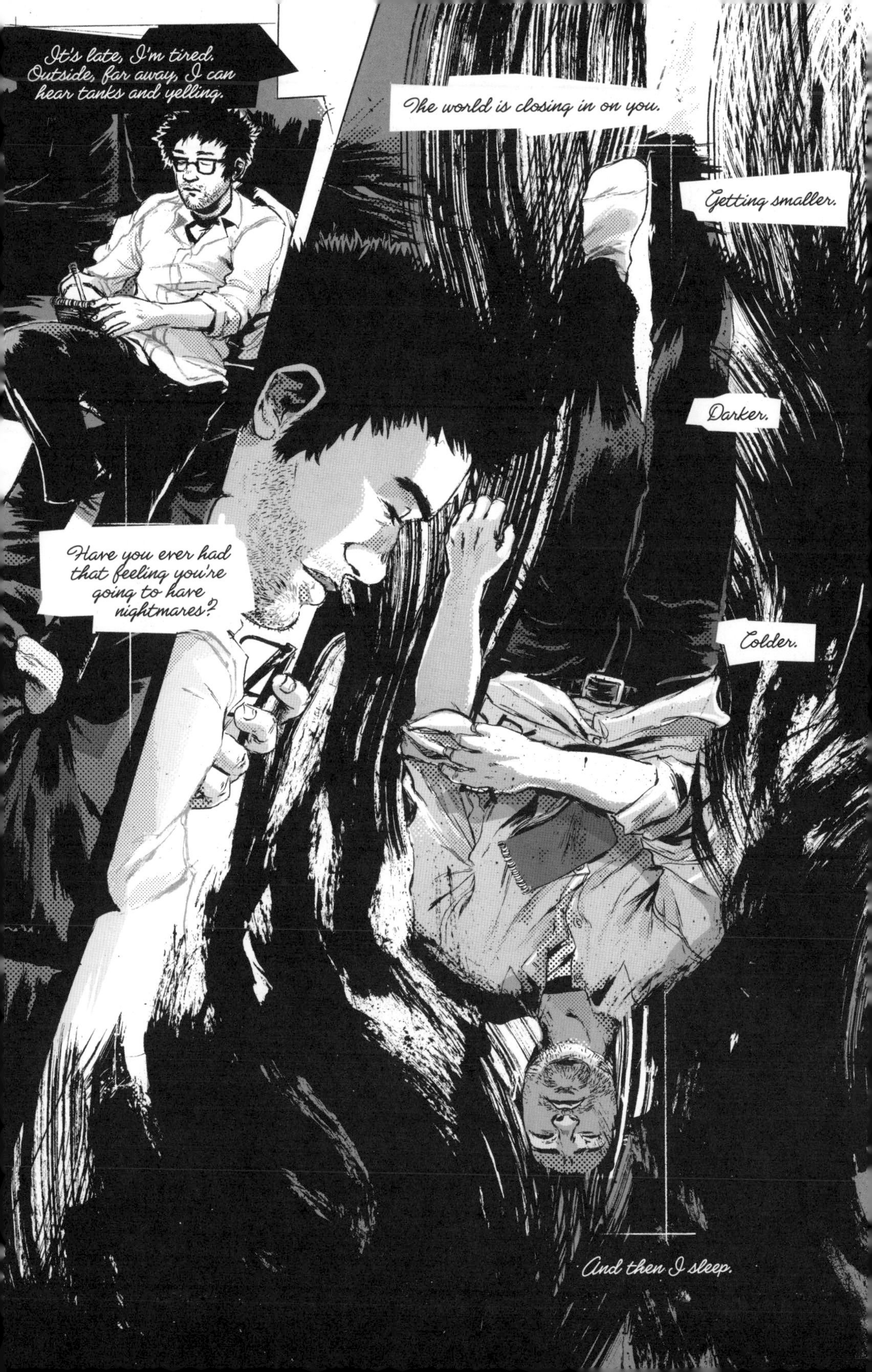
It's late, I'm tired. Outside, far away, I can hear tanks and yelling.
The world is closing in on you.
Getting smaller.
Darker.
Have you ever had that feeling you're going to have nightmares?
Colder.
And then I sleep.

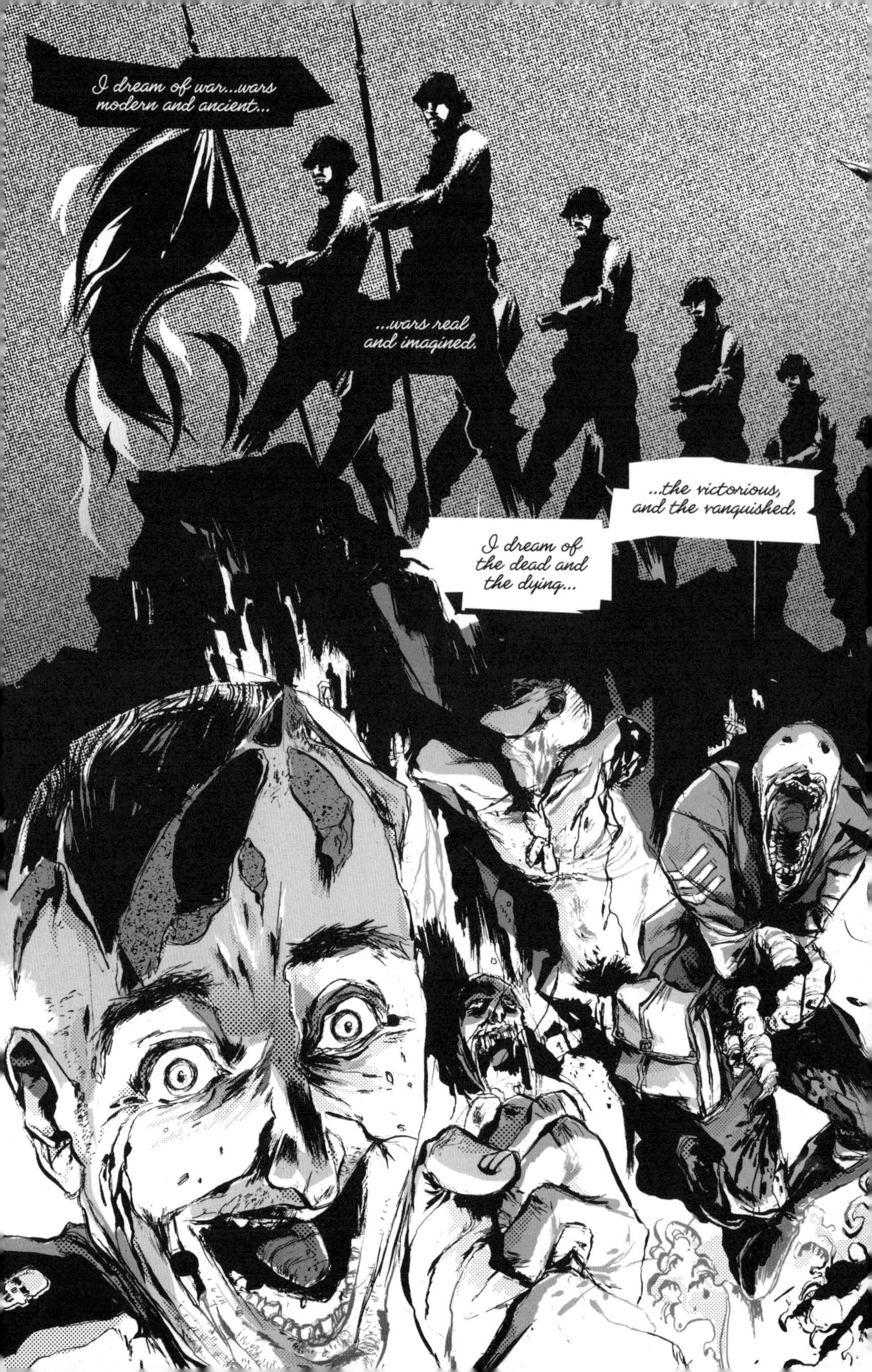
I dream of war...wars modern and ancient...
...wars real and imagined.
I dream of the dead and the dying...
...the victorious, and the vanquished.

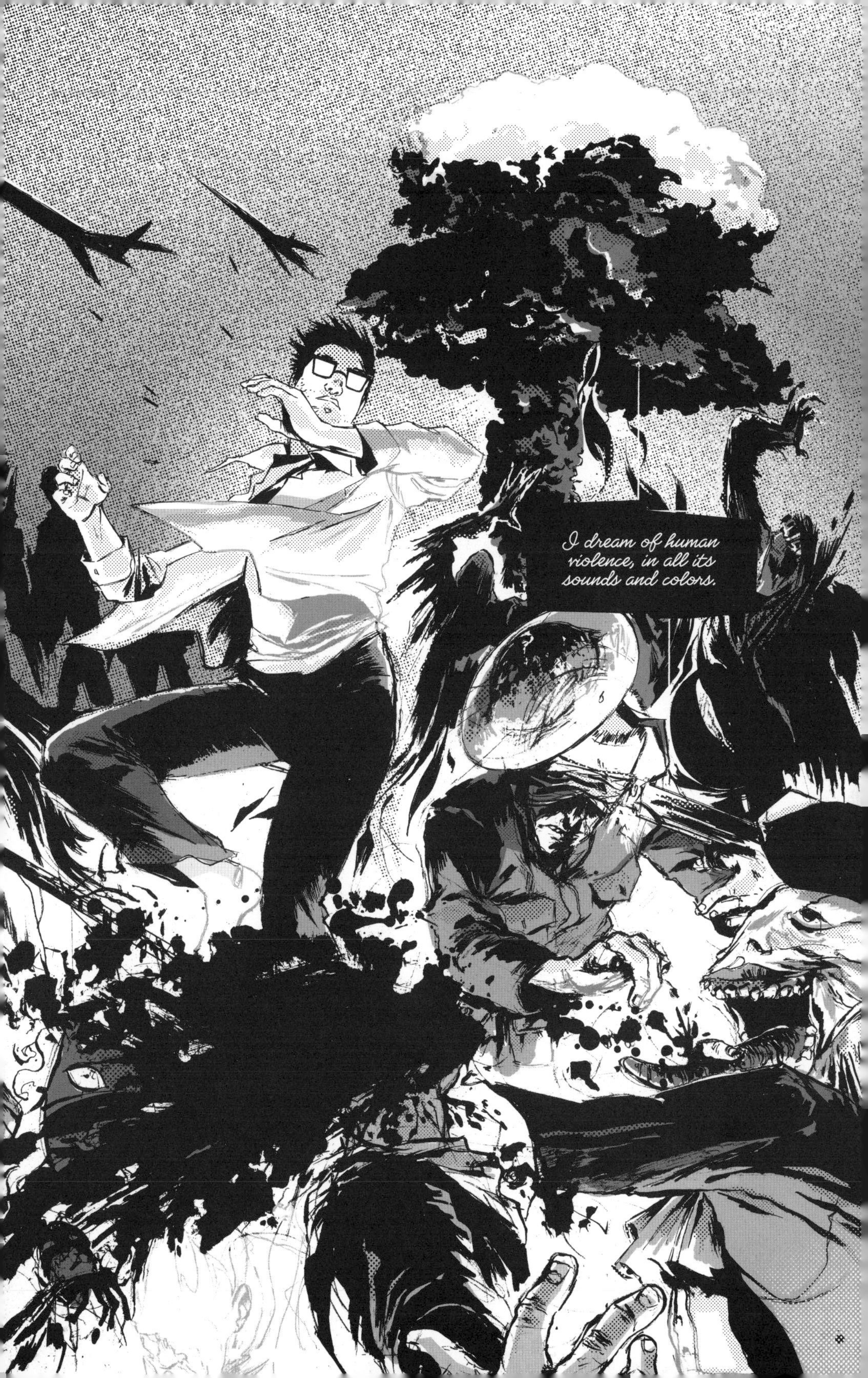
I dream of human violence, in all its sounds and colors.

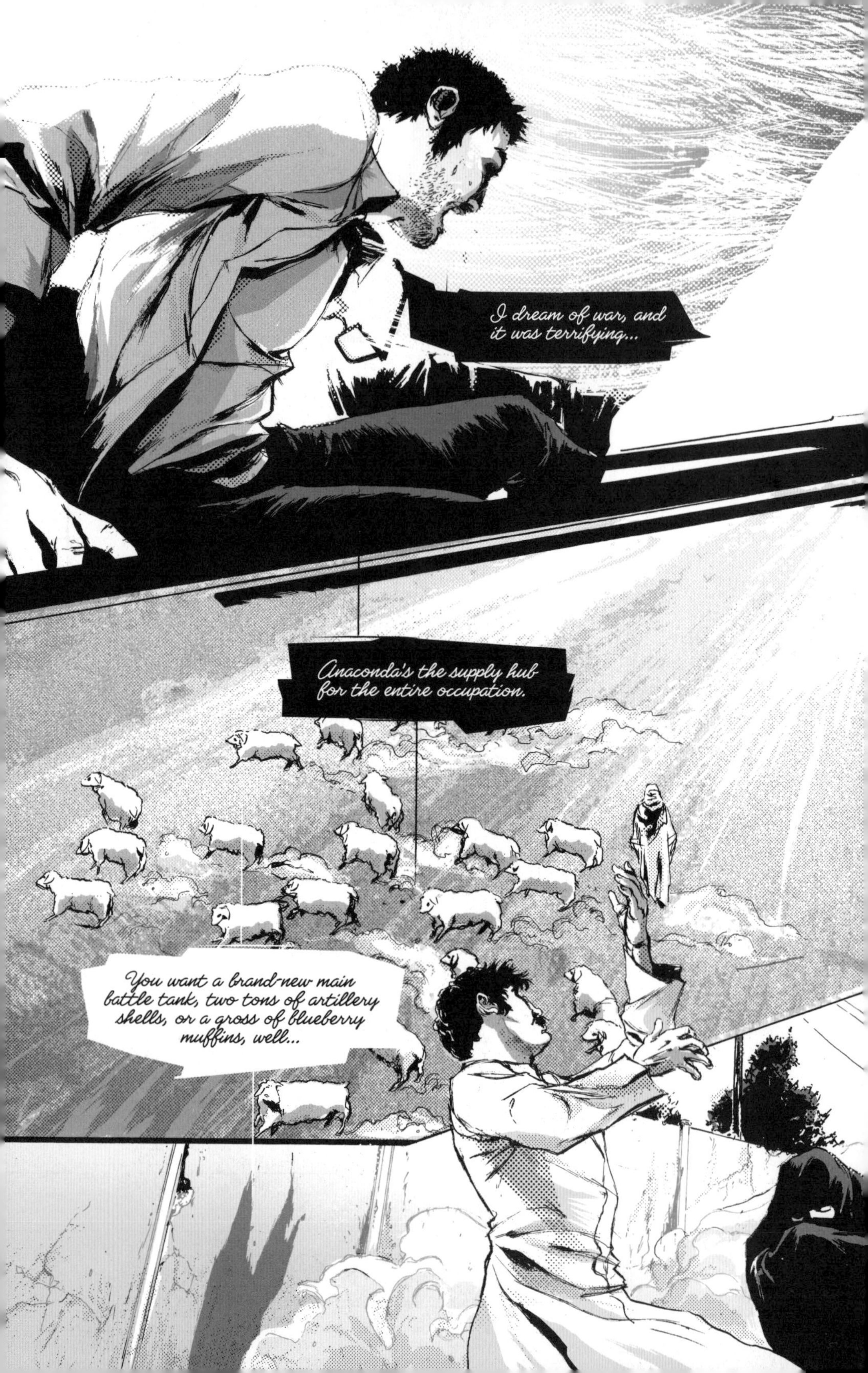
I dream of war, and it was terrifying...
Anaconda's the supply hub for the entire occupation.
You want a brand-new main battle tank, two tons of artillery shells, or a gross of blueberry muffins, well...

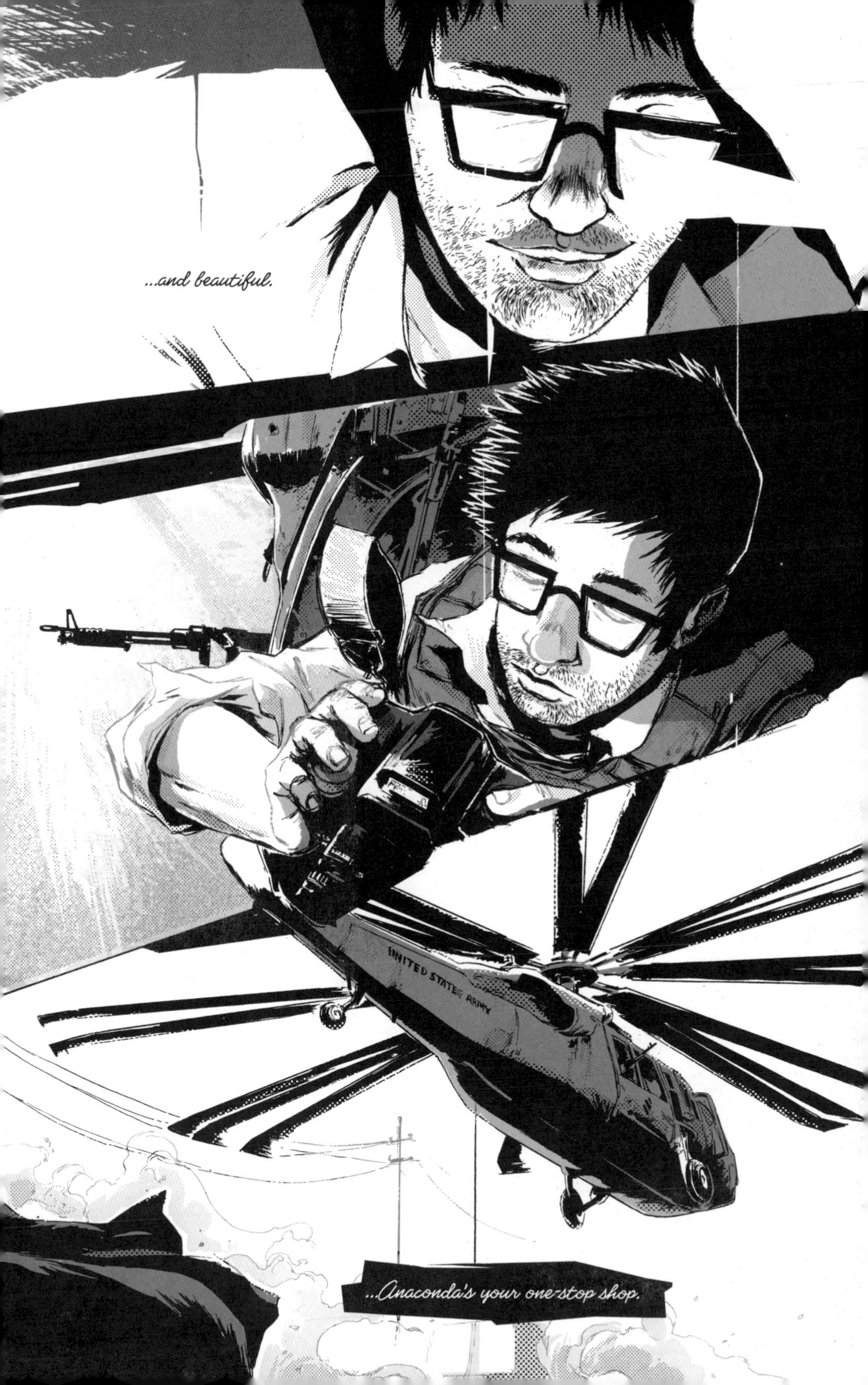
...and beautiful.
...Anaconda's your one-stop shop.
UNITED STATES ARMY

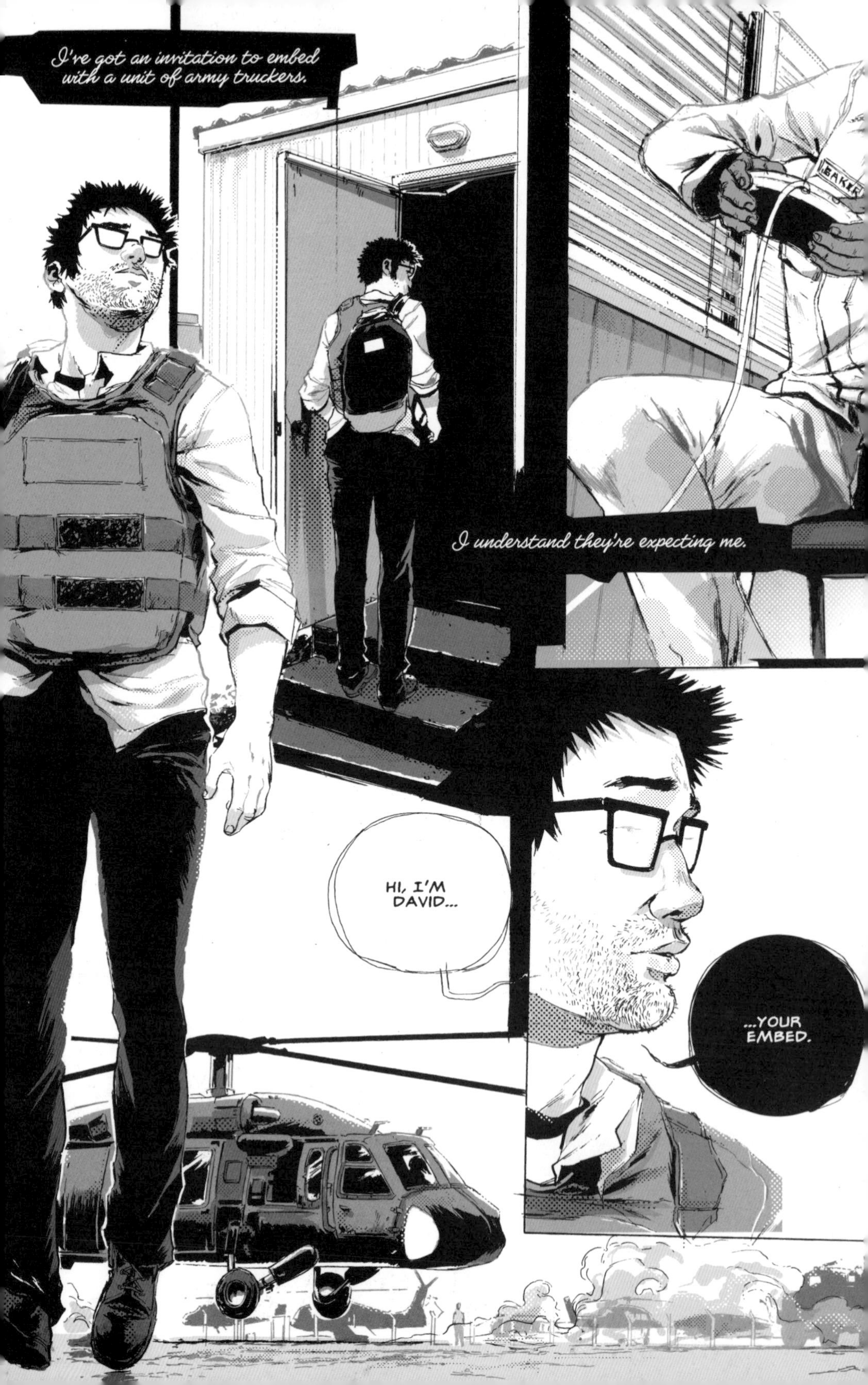
I've got an invitation to embed with a unit of army truckers.
I understand they're expecting me.
HI, I'M DAVID...
...YOUR EMBED.
BAKER

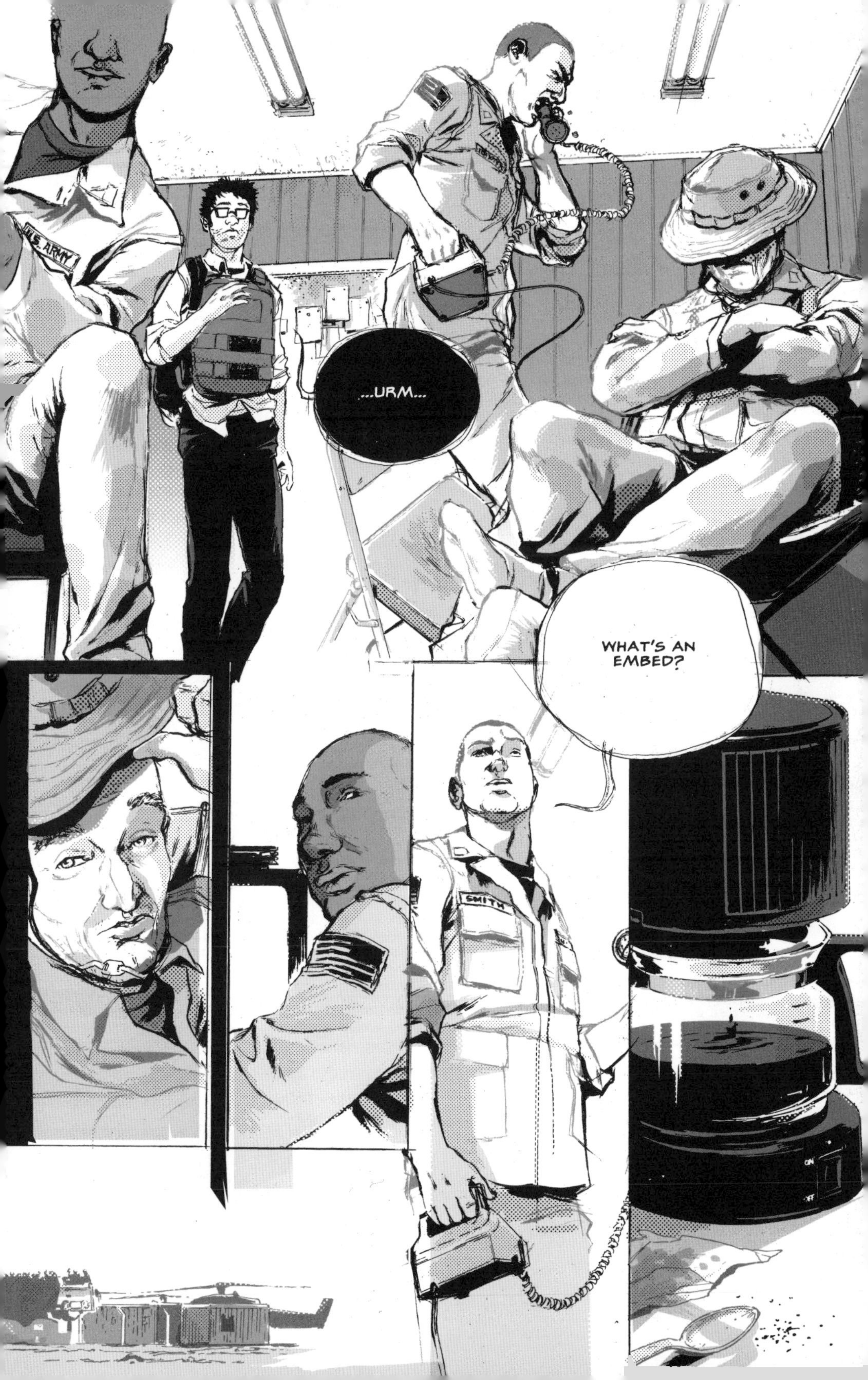

U.S. ARMY
...URM...
WHAT'S AN EMBED?
SMITH
ON
OFF

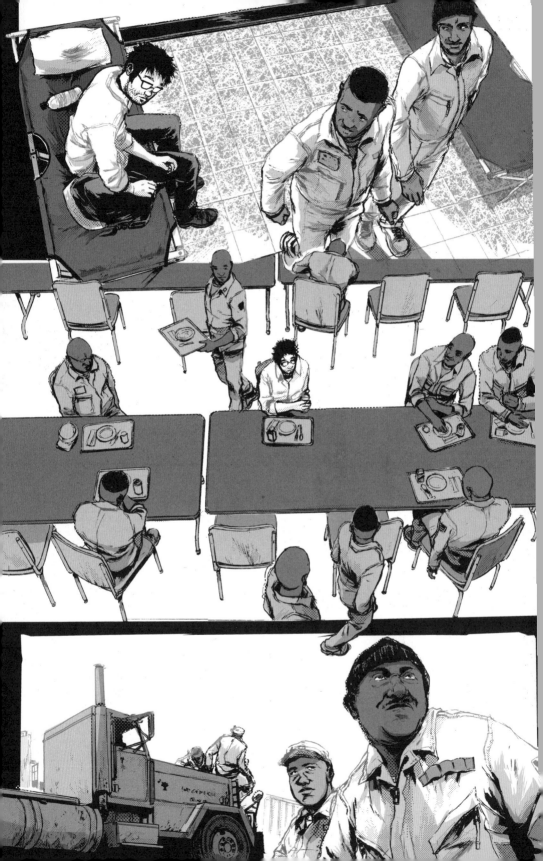

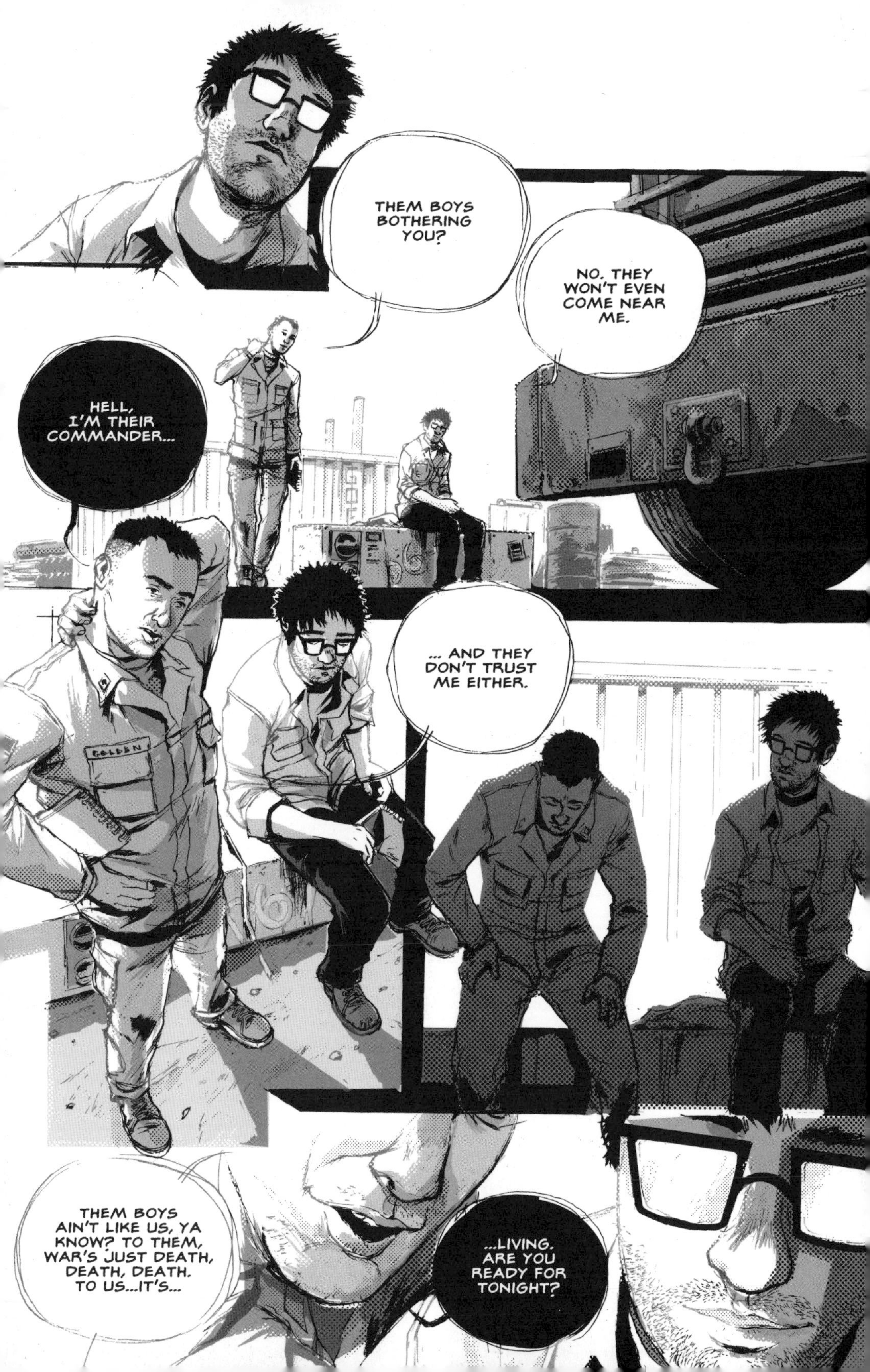
THEM BOYS BOTHERING YOU?
NO. THEY WON'T EVEN COME NEAR ME.
HELL, I'M THEIR COMMANDER...
... AND THEY DON'T TRUST ME EITHER.
GOLDEN
THEM BOYS AIN'T LIKE US, YA KNOW? TO THEM, WAR'S JUST DEATH, DEATH, DEATH. TO US...IT'S...
...LIVING. ARE YOU READY FOR TONIGHT?

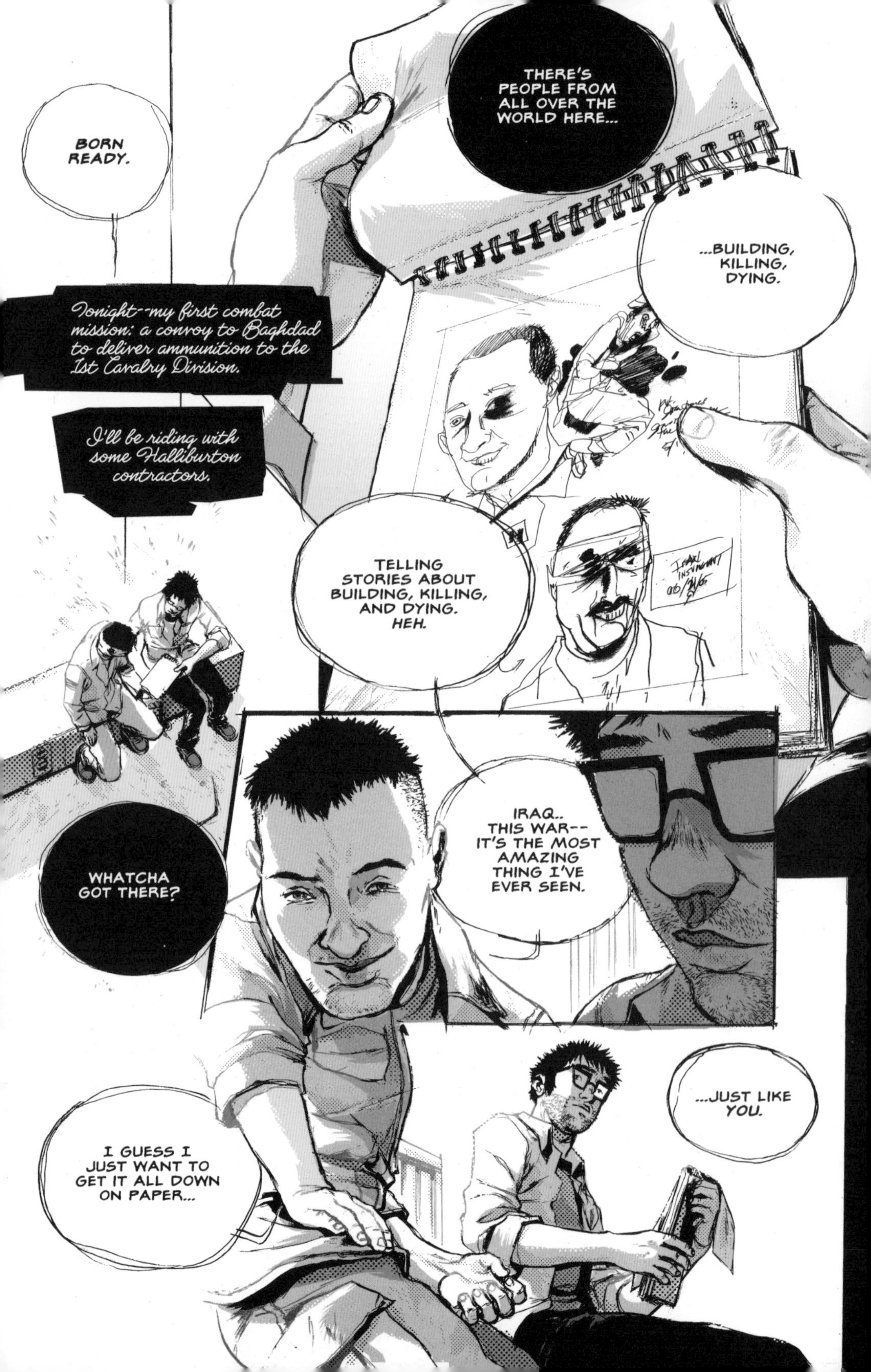

BORN READY.
THERE'S PEOPLE FROM ALL OVER THE WORLD HERE...
...BUILDING, KILLING, DYING.
Tonight--my first combat mission: a convoy to Baghdad to deliver ammunition to the 1st Cavalry Division.
I'll be riding with some Halliburton contractors.
TELLING STORIES ABOUT BUILDING, KILLING, AND DYING. HEH.
WHATCHA GOT THERE?
IRAQ.. THIS WAR-- IT'S THE MOST AMAZING THING I'VE EVER SEEN.
...JUST LIKE YOU.
I GUESS I JUST WANT TO GET IT ALL DOWN ON PAPER...

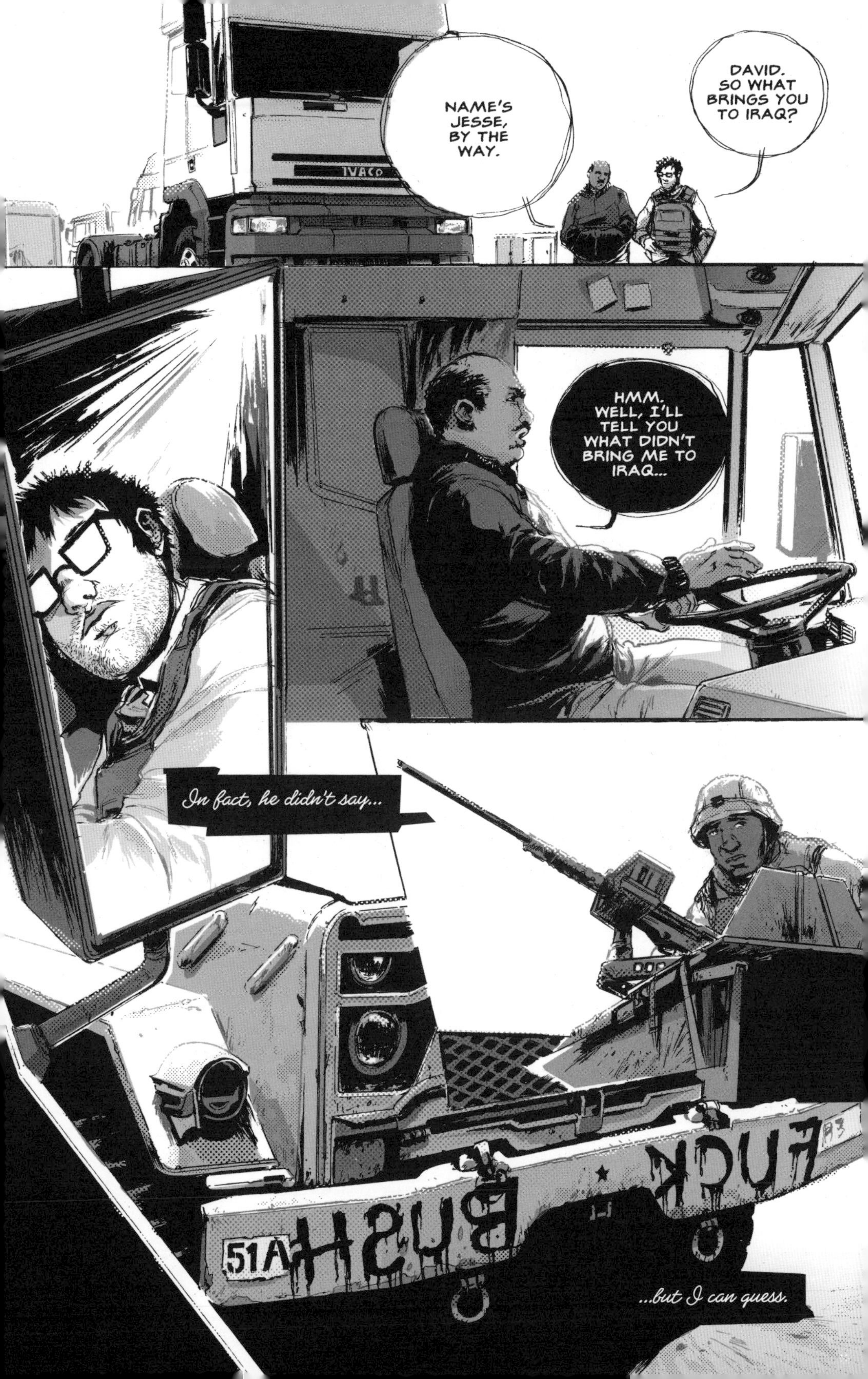
NAME'S JESSE, BY THE WAY.
DAVID. SO WHAT BRINGS YOU TO IRAQ?
HMM. WELL, I'LL TELL YOU WHAT DIDN'T BRING ME TO IRAQ...
In fact, he didn't say...
...but I can guess.

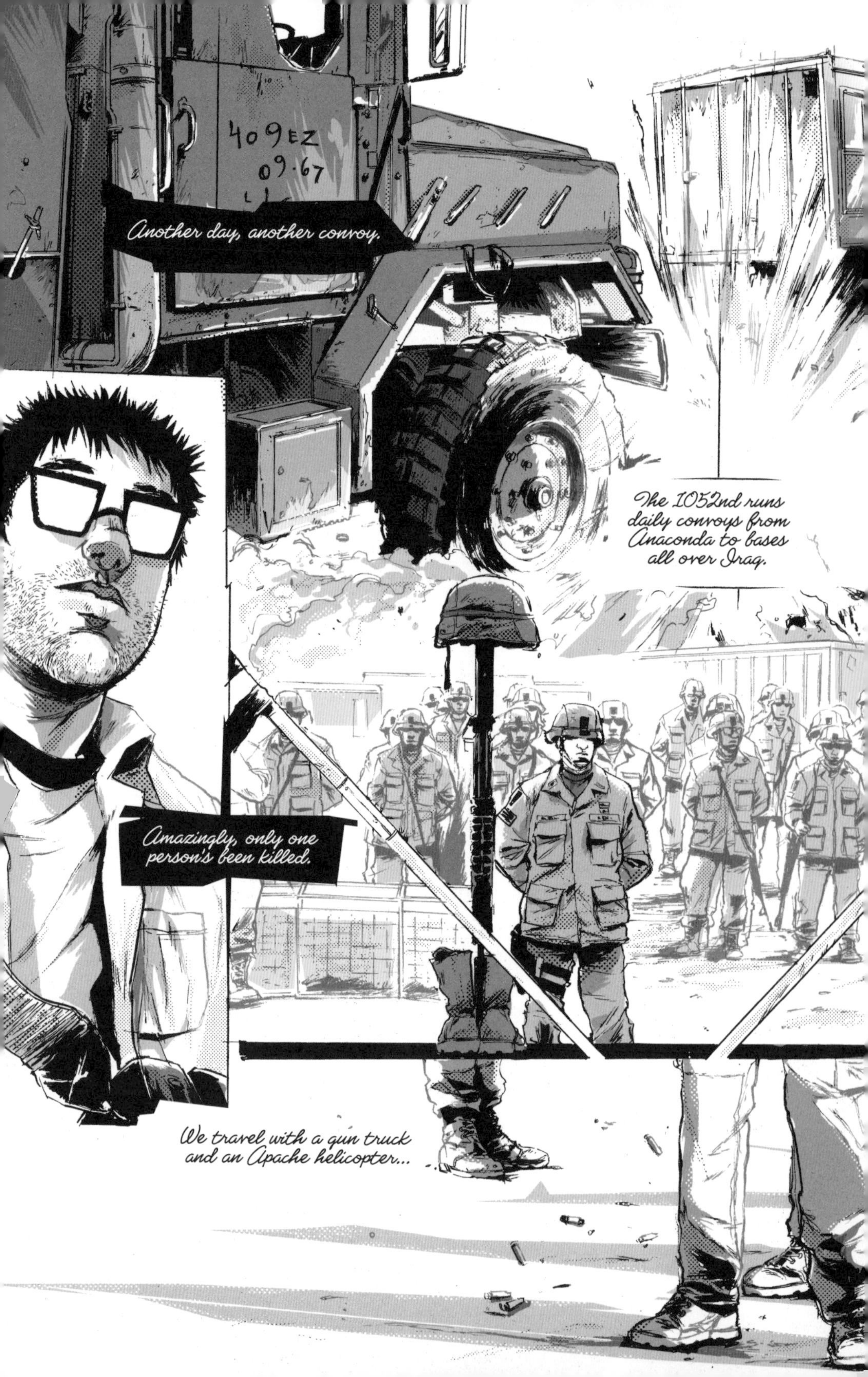
409EZ
09·67
Another day, another convoy.
The 1052nd runs daily convoys from Anaconda to bases all over Iraq.
Amazingly, only one person's been killed.
We travel with a gun truck and an Apache helicopter...

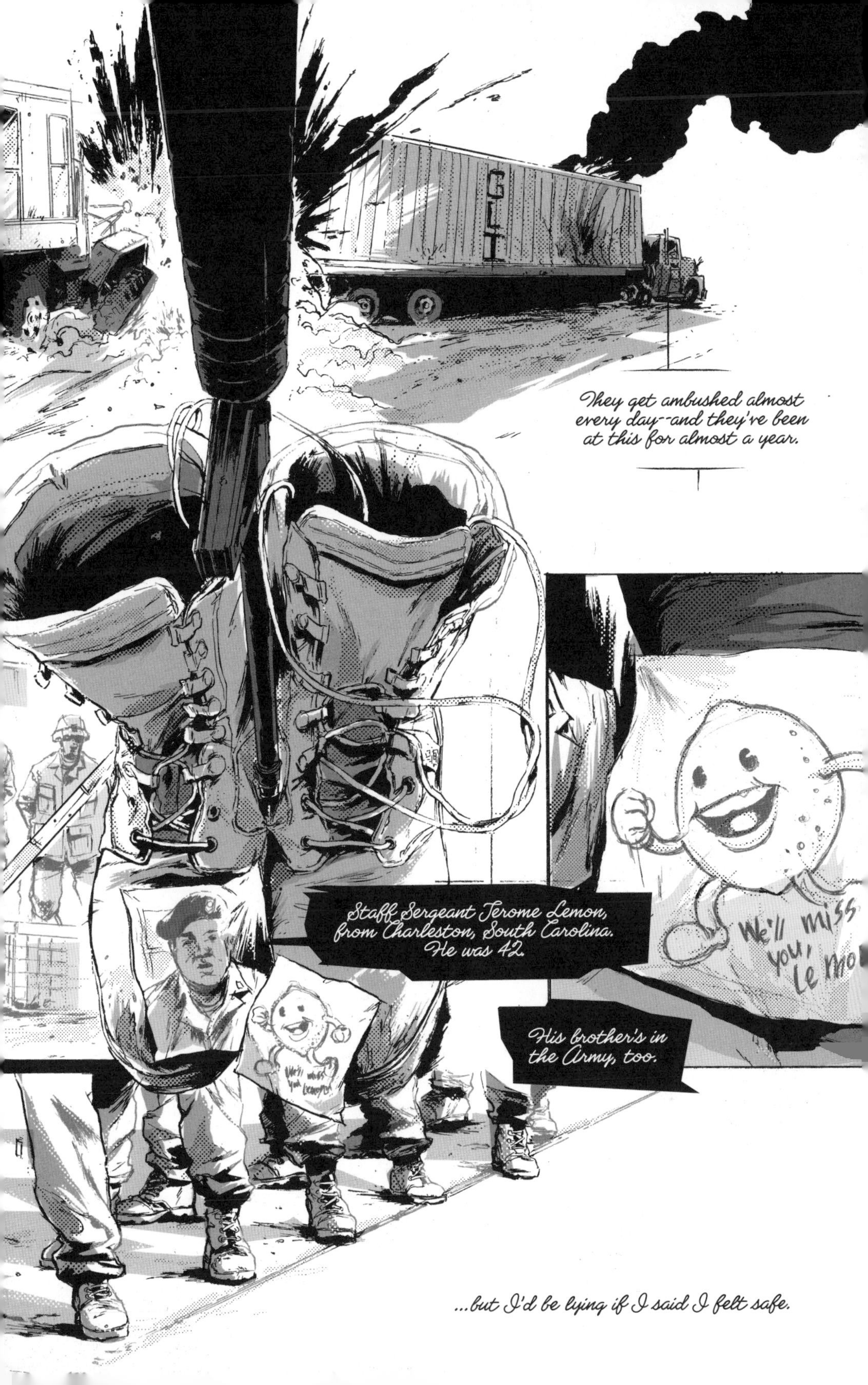
GLT
They get ambushed almost every day--and they've been at this for almost a year.
Staff Sergeant Jerome Lemon, from Charleston, South Carolina. He was 42.
We'll miss you,
His brother's in the Army, too.
...but I'd be lying if I said I felt safe.

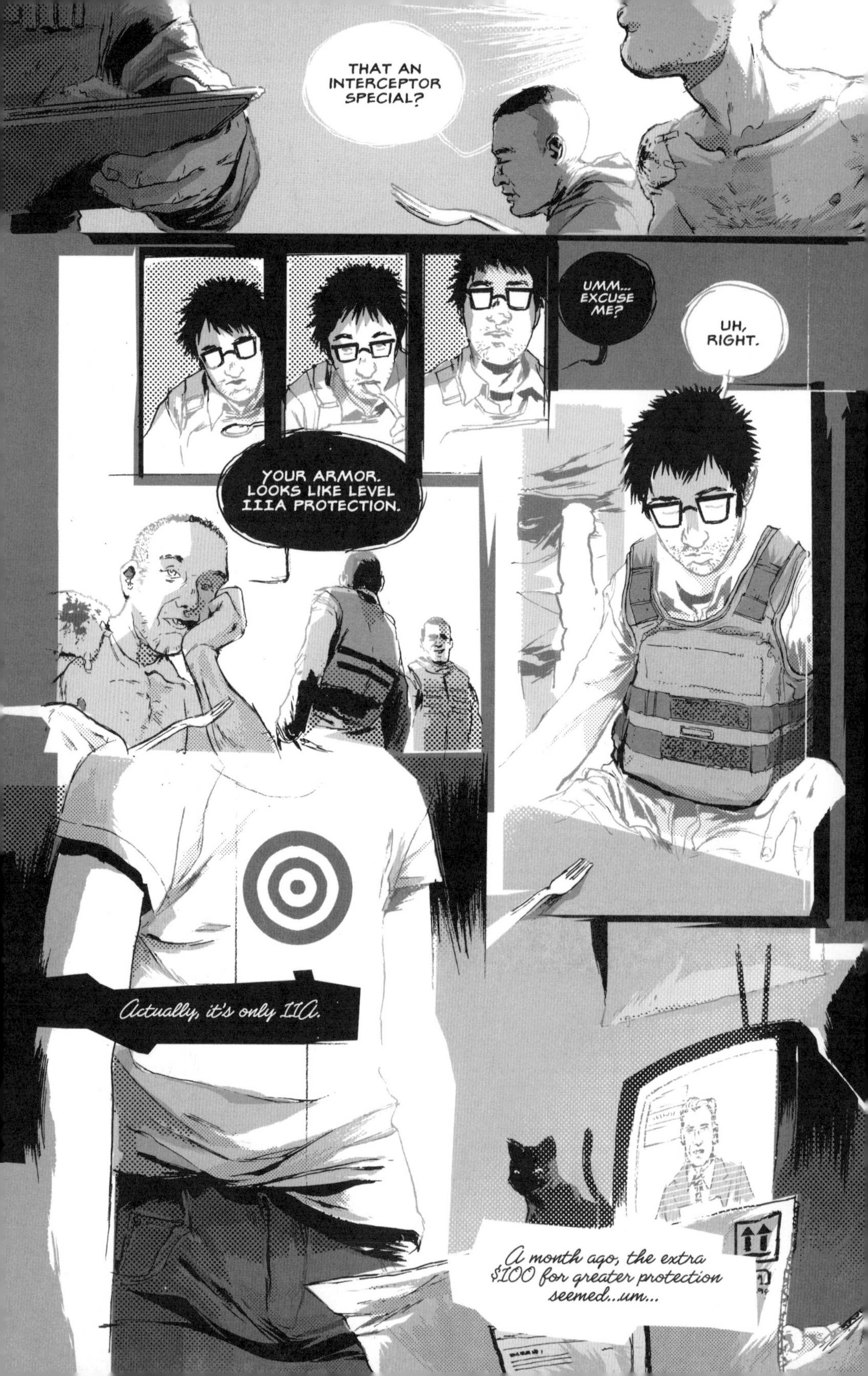
THAT AN INTERCEPTOR SPECIAL?
UMM... EXCUSE ME?
YOUR ARMOR. LOOKS LIKE LEVEL IIIA PROTECTION.
UH, RIGHT.
Actually, it's only IIA.
A month ago, the extra $100 for greater protection seemed...um...

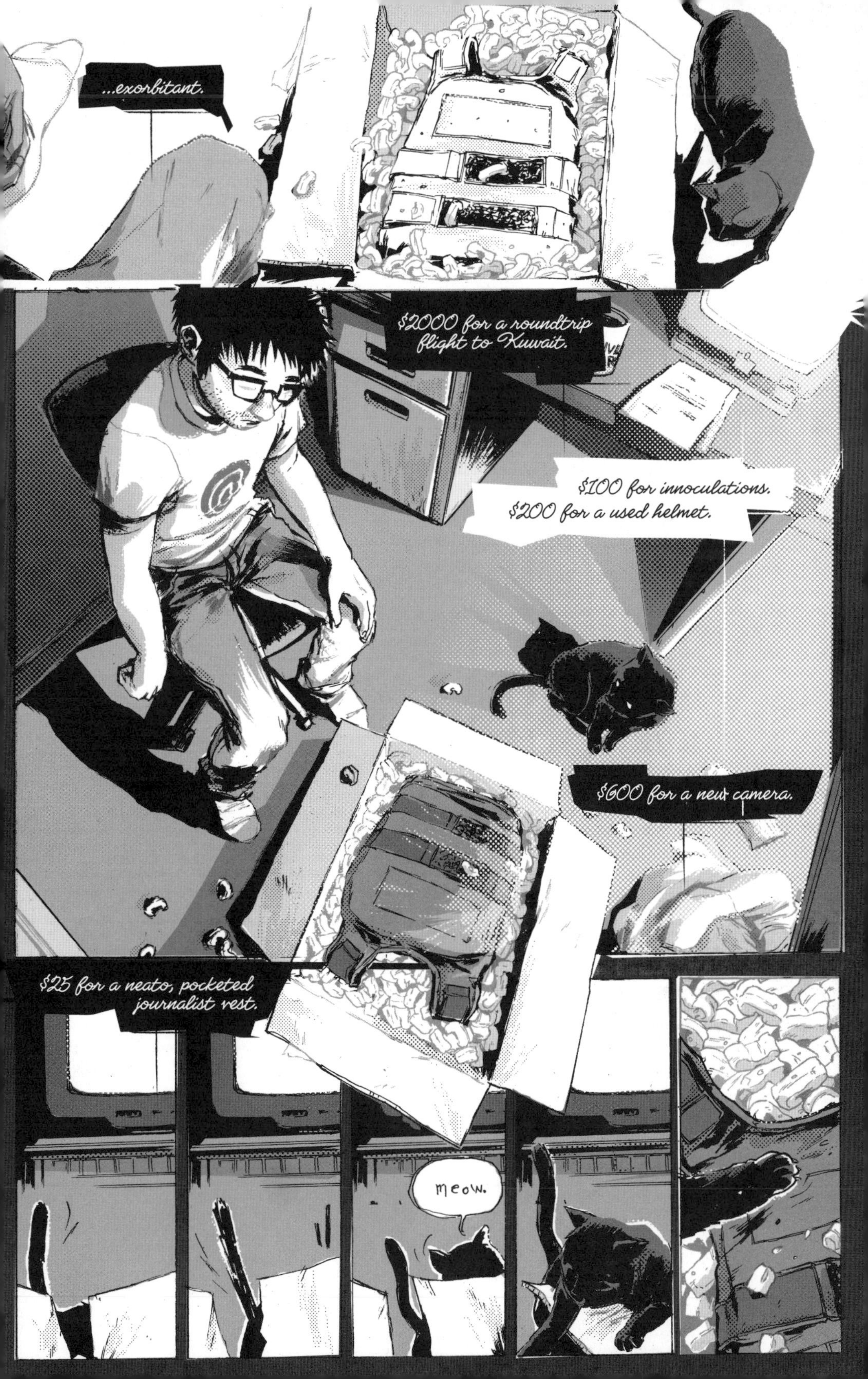
...exorbitant.
$2000 for a roundtrip flight to Kuwait.
$100 for innoculations.
$200 for a used helmet.
$600 for a new camera.
$25 for a neato, pocketed journalist vest.
meow.

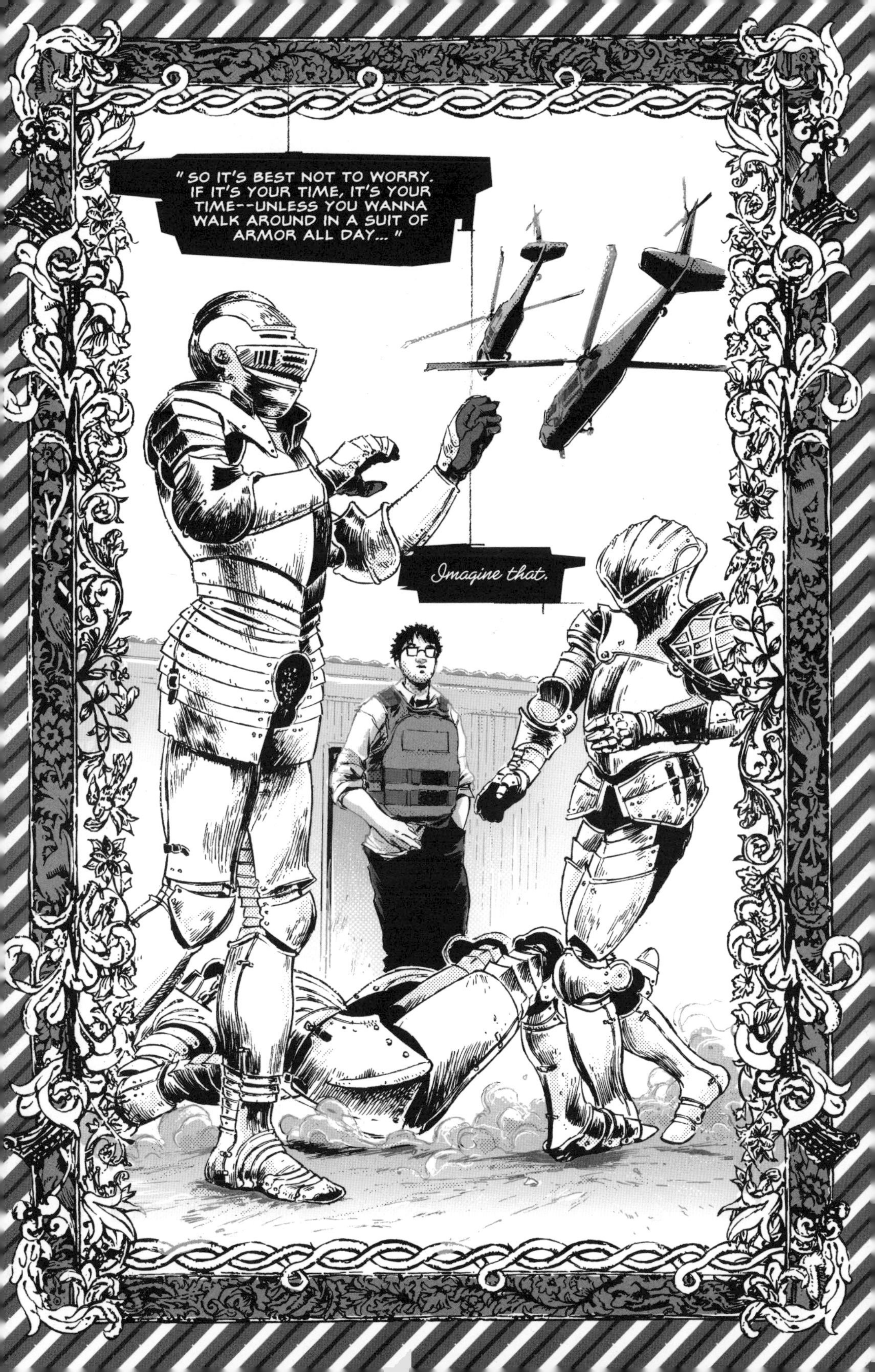
"SO IT'S BEST NOT TO WORRY. IF IT'S YOUR TIME, IT'S YOUR TIME--UNLESS YOU WANNA WALK AROUND IN A SUIT OF ARMOR ALL DAY..."
Imagine that.

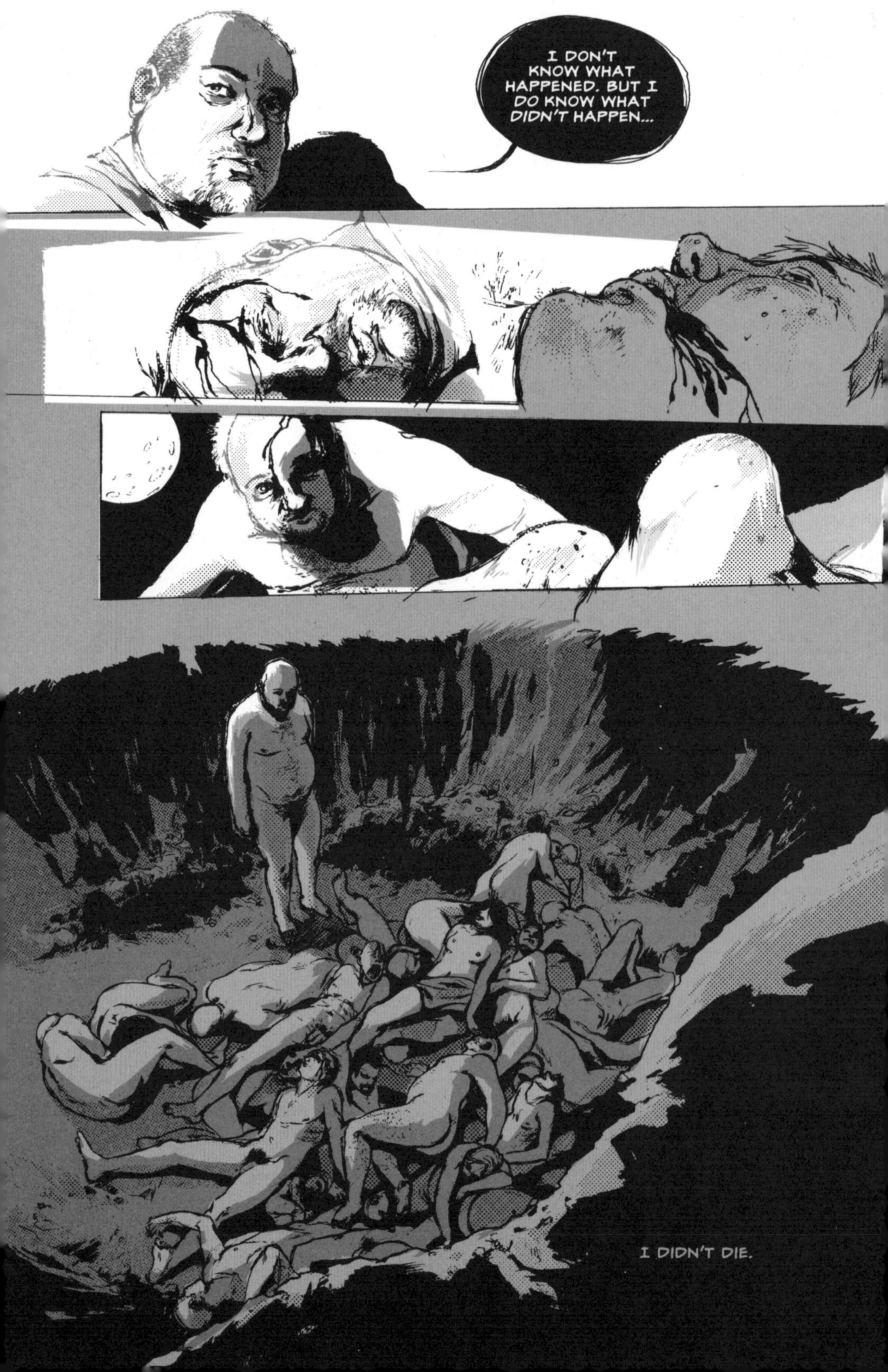
I DON'T KNOW WHAT HAPPENED. BUT I DO KNOW WHAT DIDN'T HAPPEN...
I DIDN'T DIE.

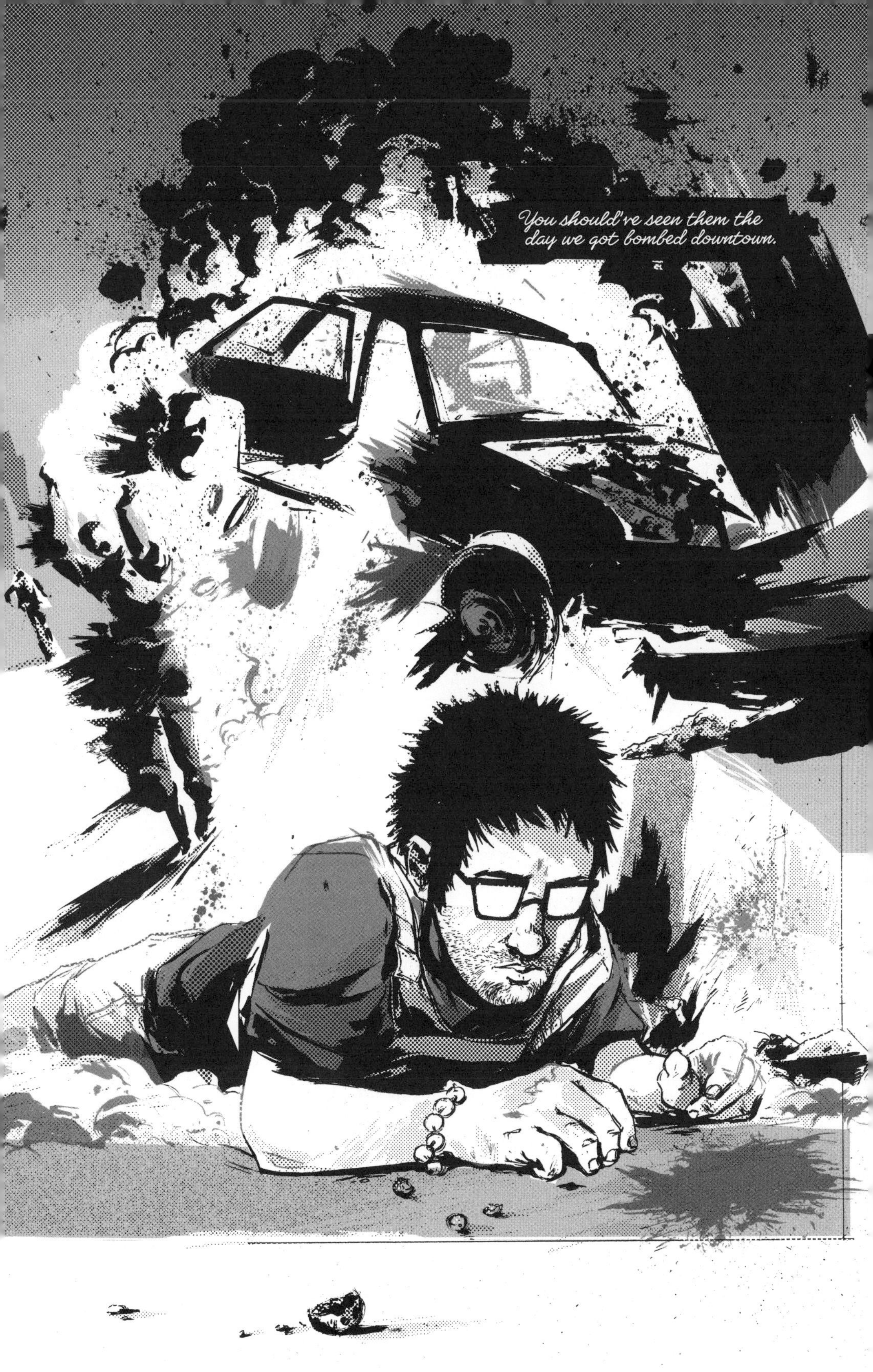
You should've seen them the day we got bombed downtown.

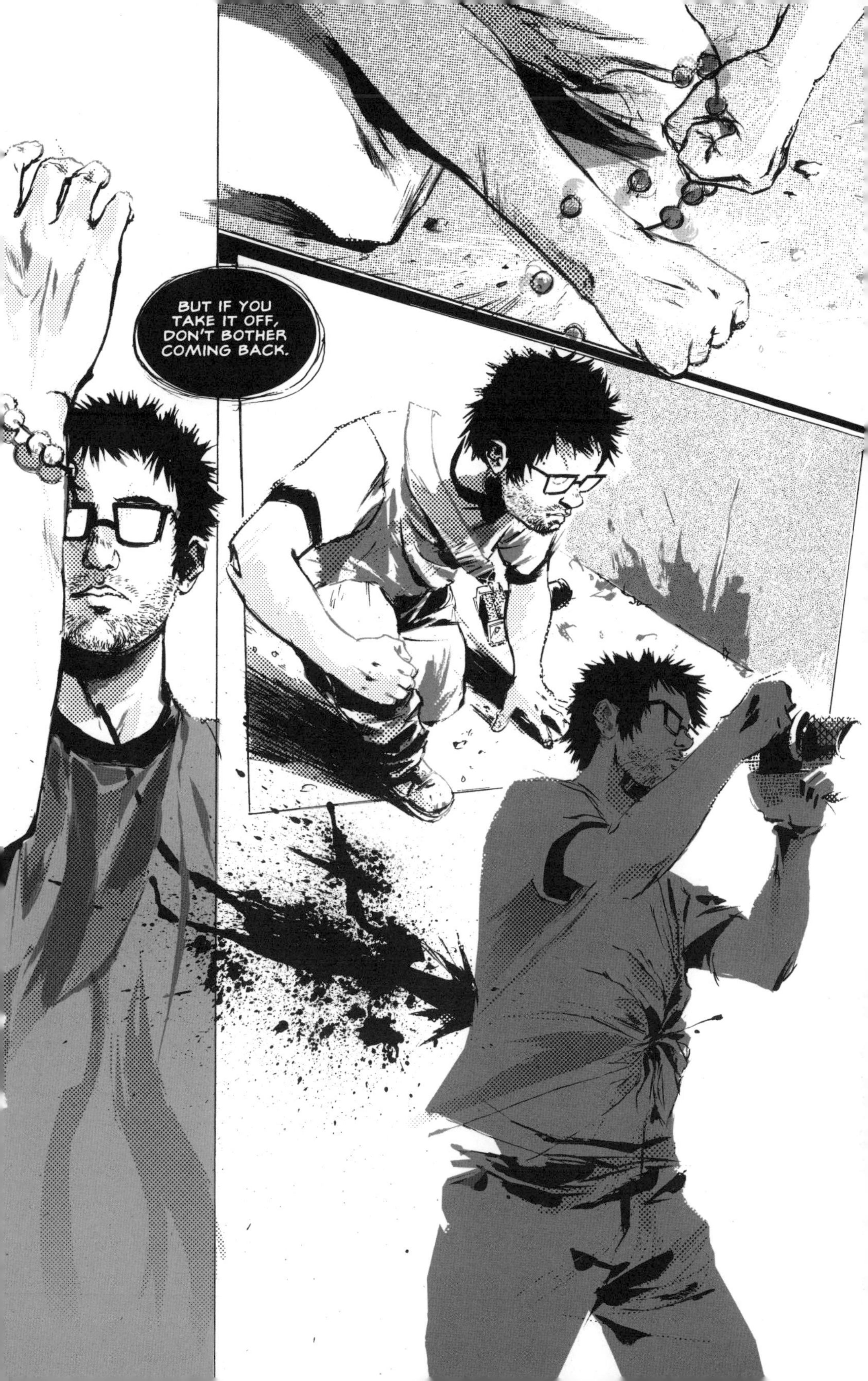
BUT IF YOU TAKE IT OFF, DON'T BOTHER COMING BACK.

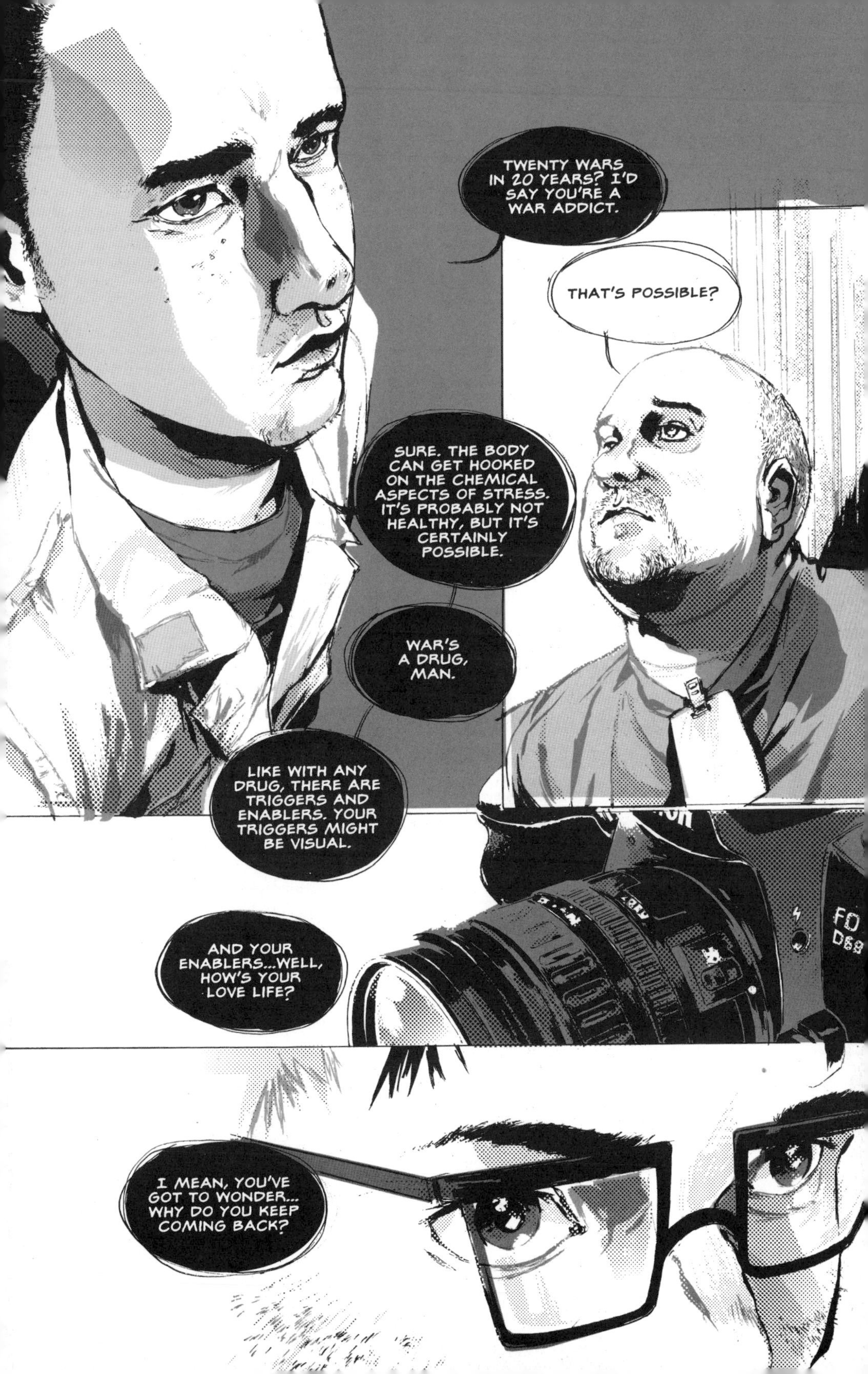
TWENTY WARS IN 20 YEARS? I'D SAY YOU'RE A WAR ADDICT.
THAT'S POSSIBLE?
SURE. THE BODY CAN GET HOOKED ON THE CHEMICAL ASPECTS OF STRESS. IT'S PROBABLY NOT HEALTHY, BUT IT'S CERTAINLY POSSIBLE.
WAR'S A DRUG, MAN.
LIKE WITH ANY DRUG, THERE ARE TRIGGERS AND ENABLERS. YOUR TRIGGERS MIGHT BE VISUAL.
AND YOUR ENABLERS...WELL, HOW'S YOUR LOVE LIFE?
I MEAN, YOU'VE GOT TO WONDER... WHY DO YOU KEEP COMING BACK?

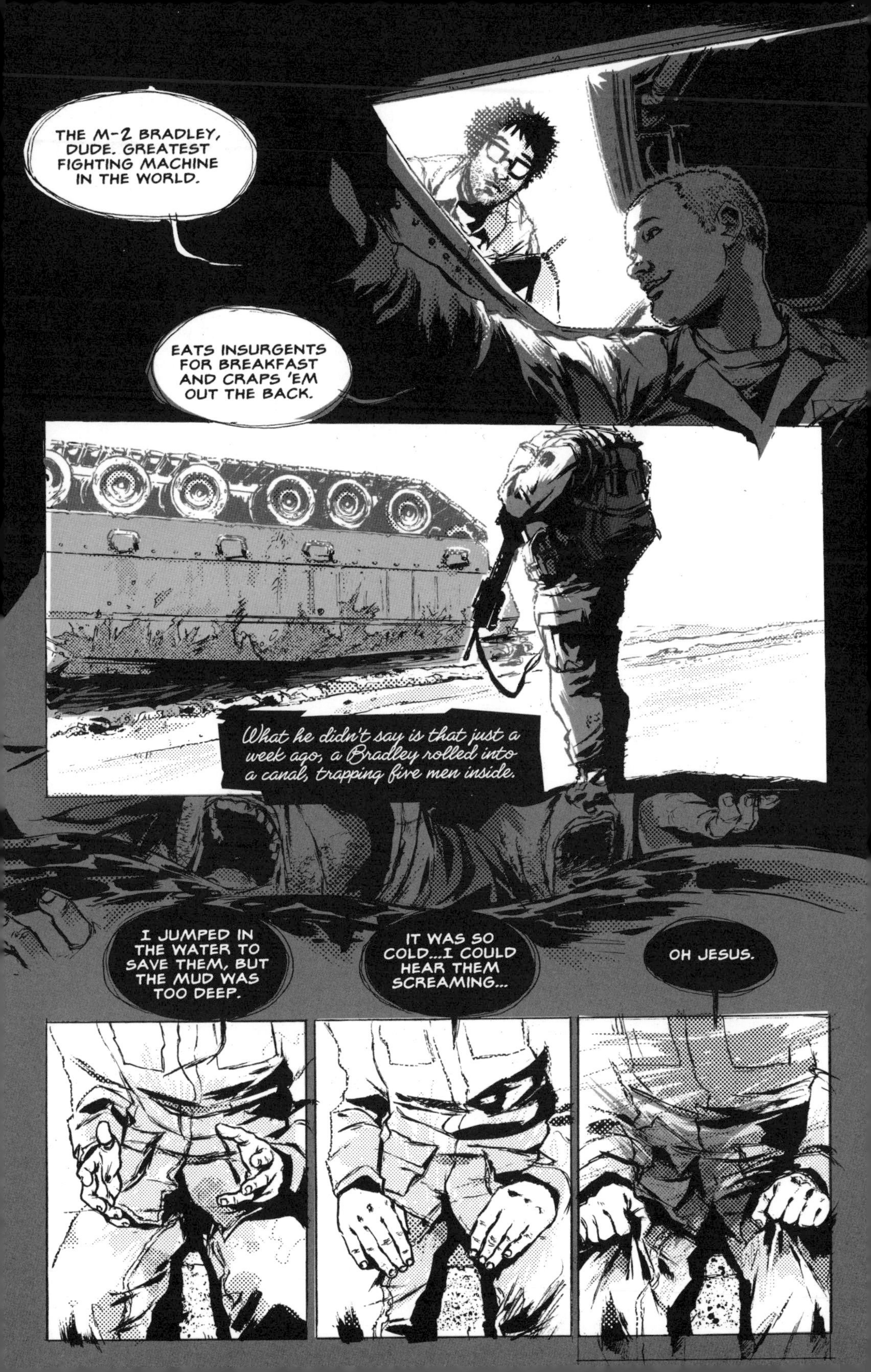
THE M-2 BRADLEY, DUDE. GREATEST FIGHTING MACHINE IN THE WORLD.
EATS INSURGENTS FOR BREAKFAST AND CRAPS 'EM OUT THE BACK.
What he didn't say is that just a week ago, a Bradley rolled into a canal, trapping five men inside.
I JUMPED IN THE WATER TO SAVE THEM, BUT THE MUD WAS TOO DEEP.
IT WAS SO COLD...I COULD HEAR THEM SCREAMING...
OH JESUS.

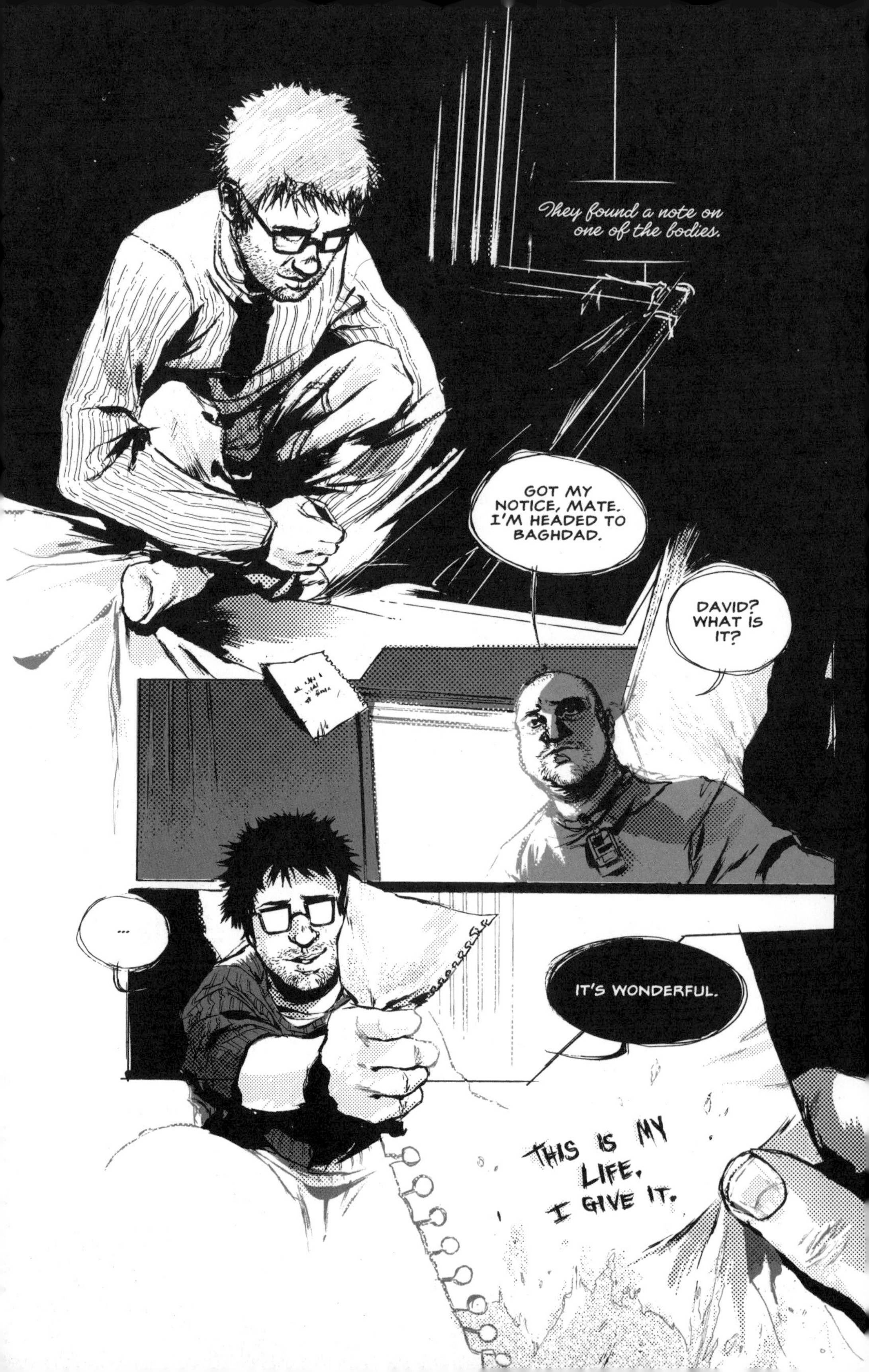
They found a note on one of the bodies.
GOT MY NOTICE, MATE. I'M HEADED TO BAGHDAD.
DAVID? WHAT IS IT?
...
IT'S WONDERFUL.
THIS IS MY LIFE. I GIVE IT.

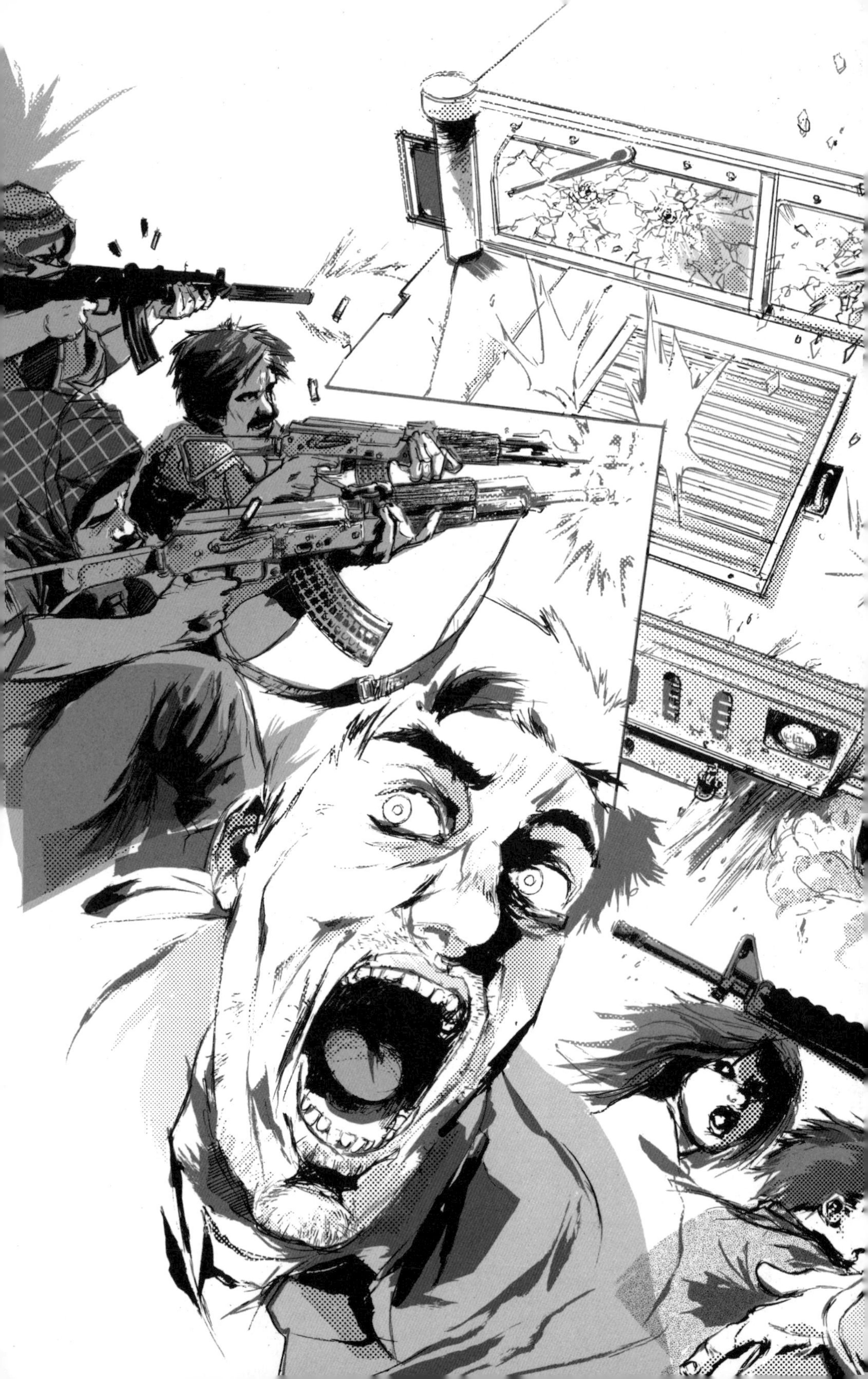

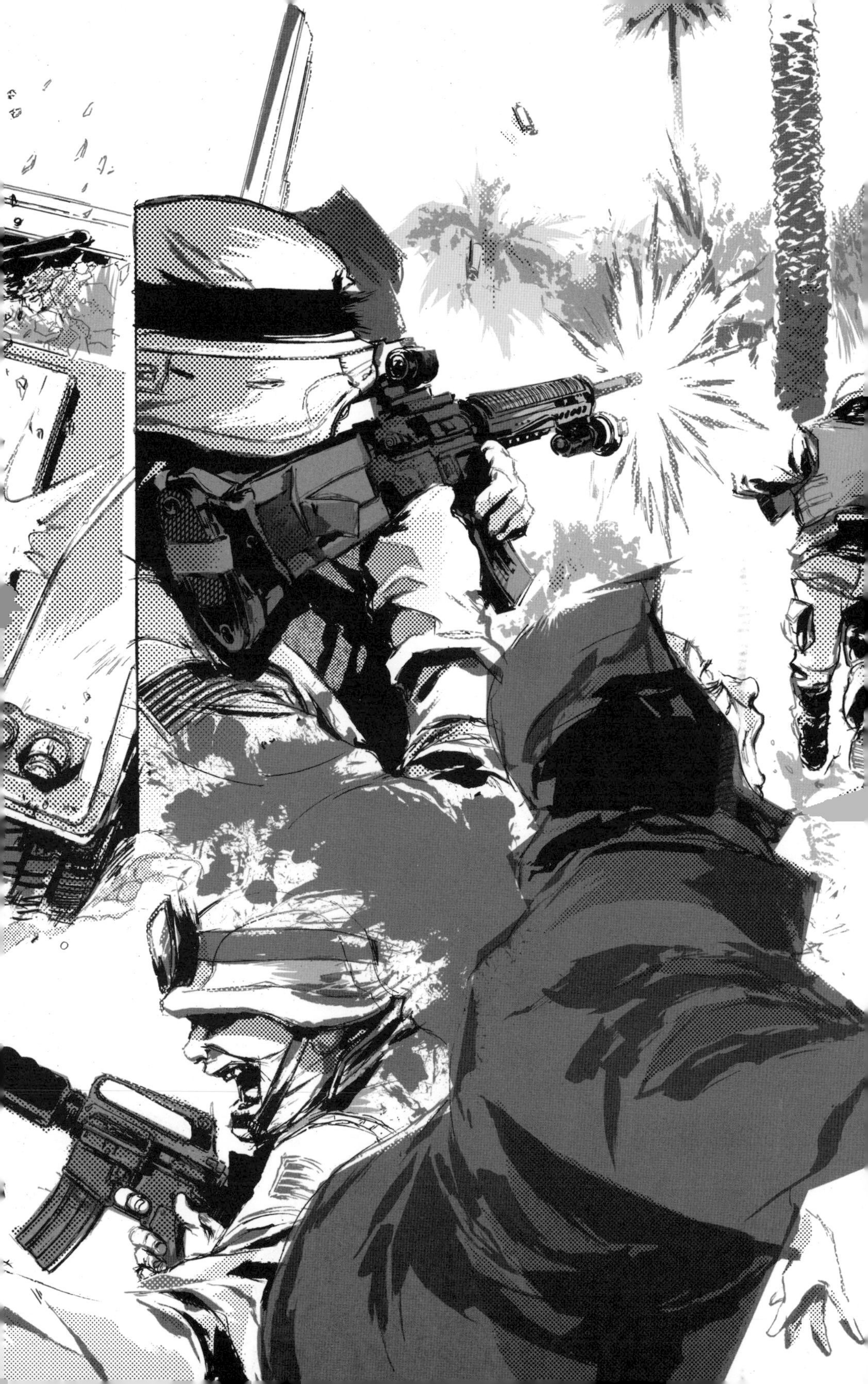

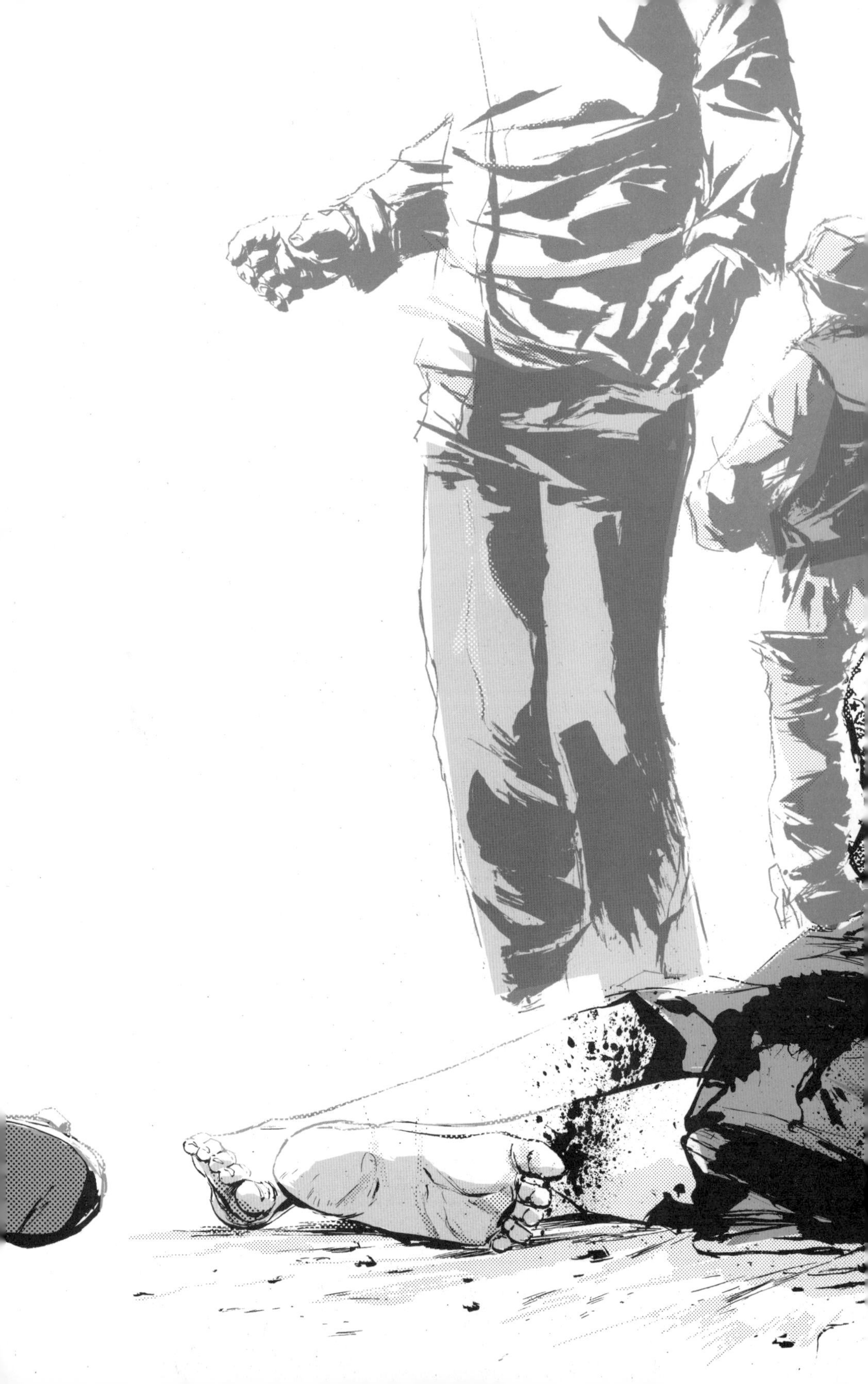

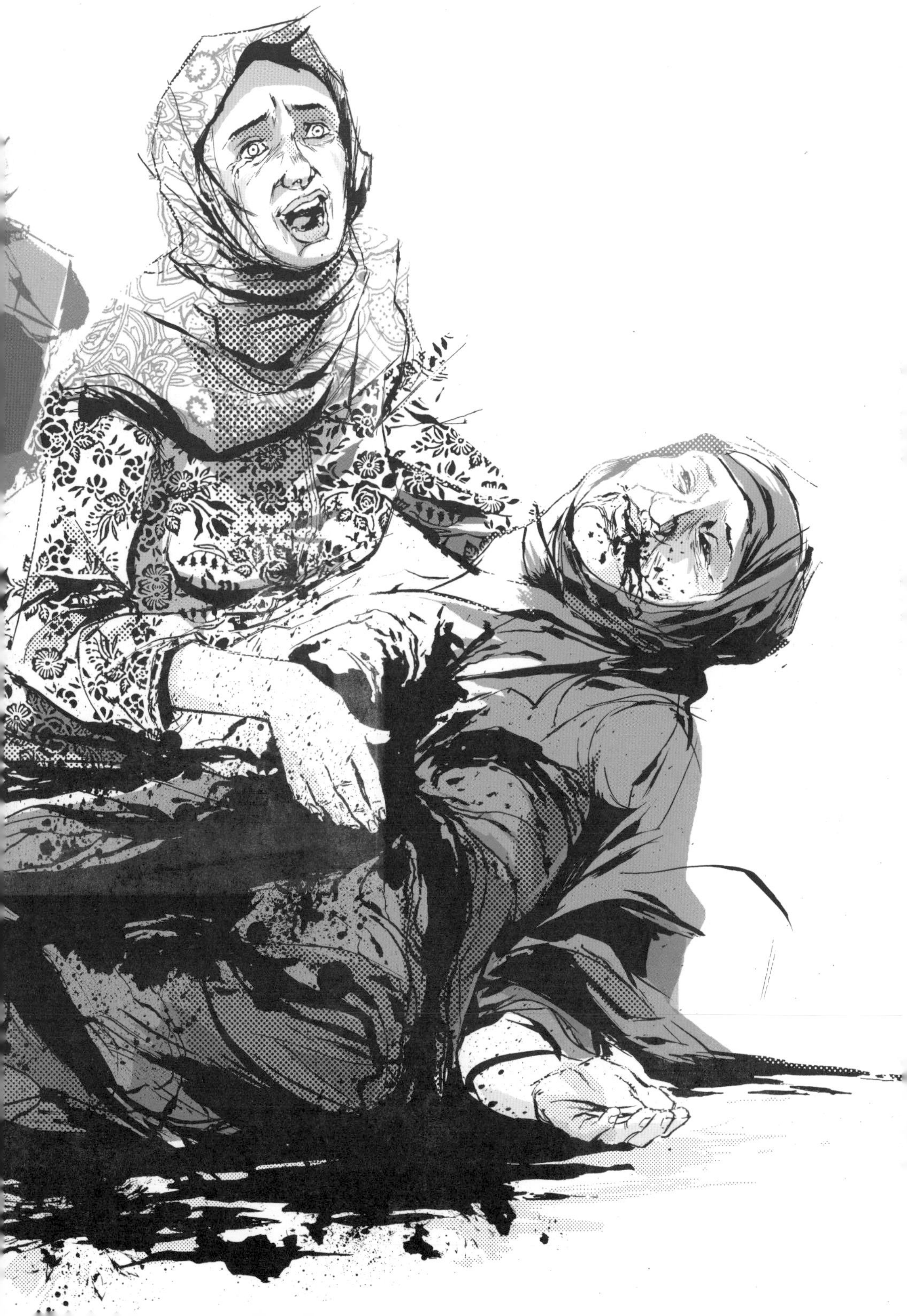

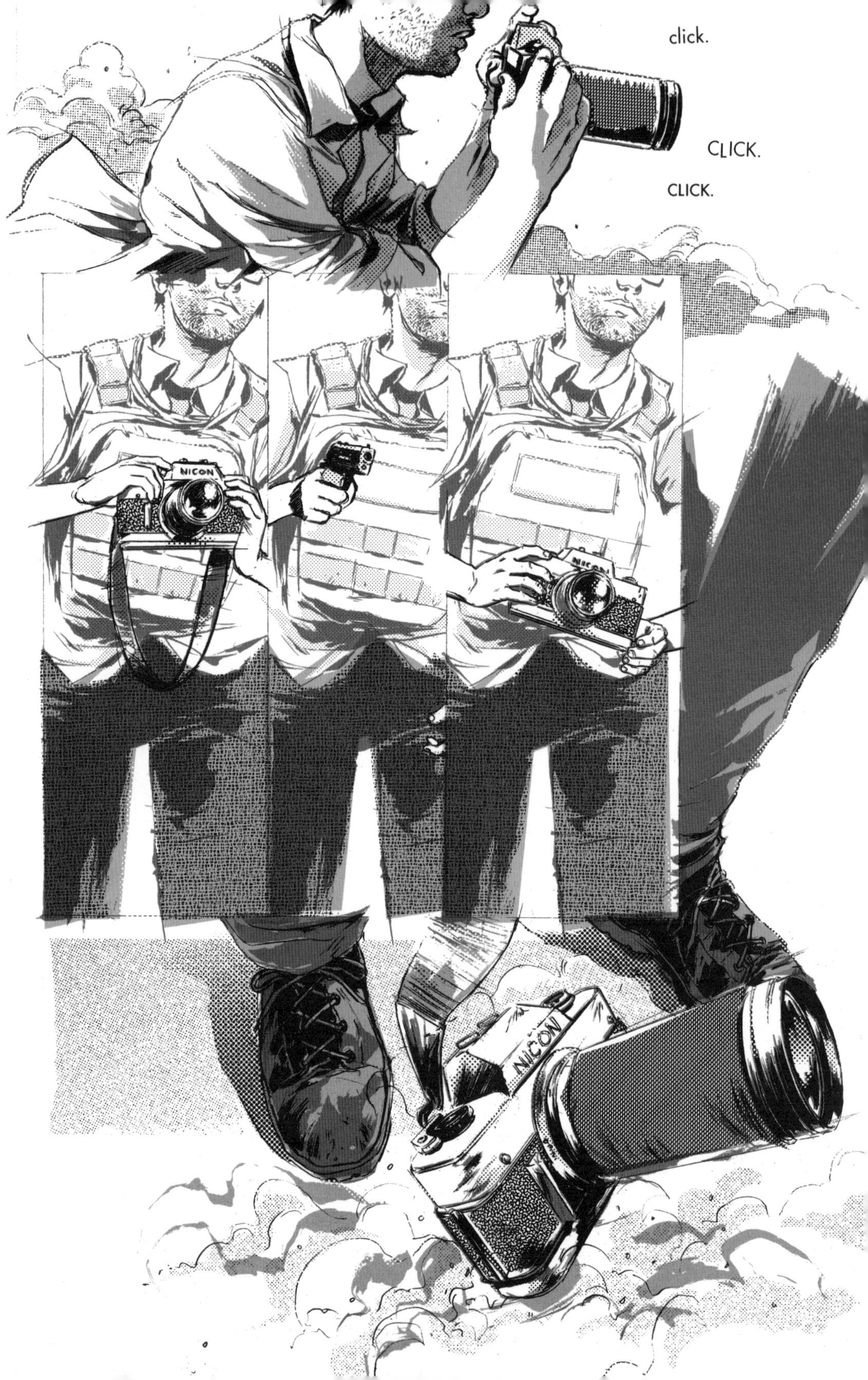
click.
CLICK.
CLICK.
NICON
NICON
NICON

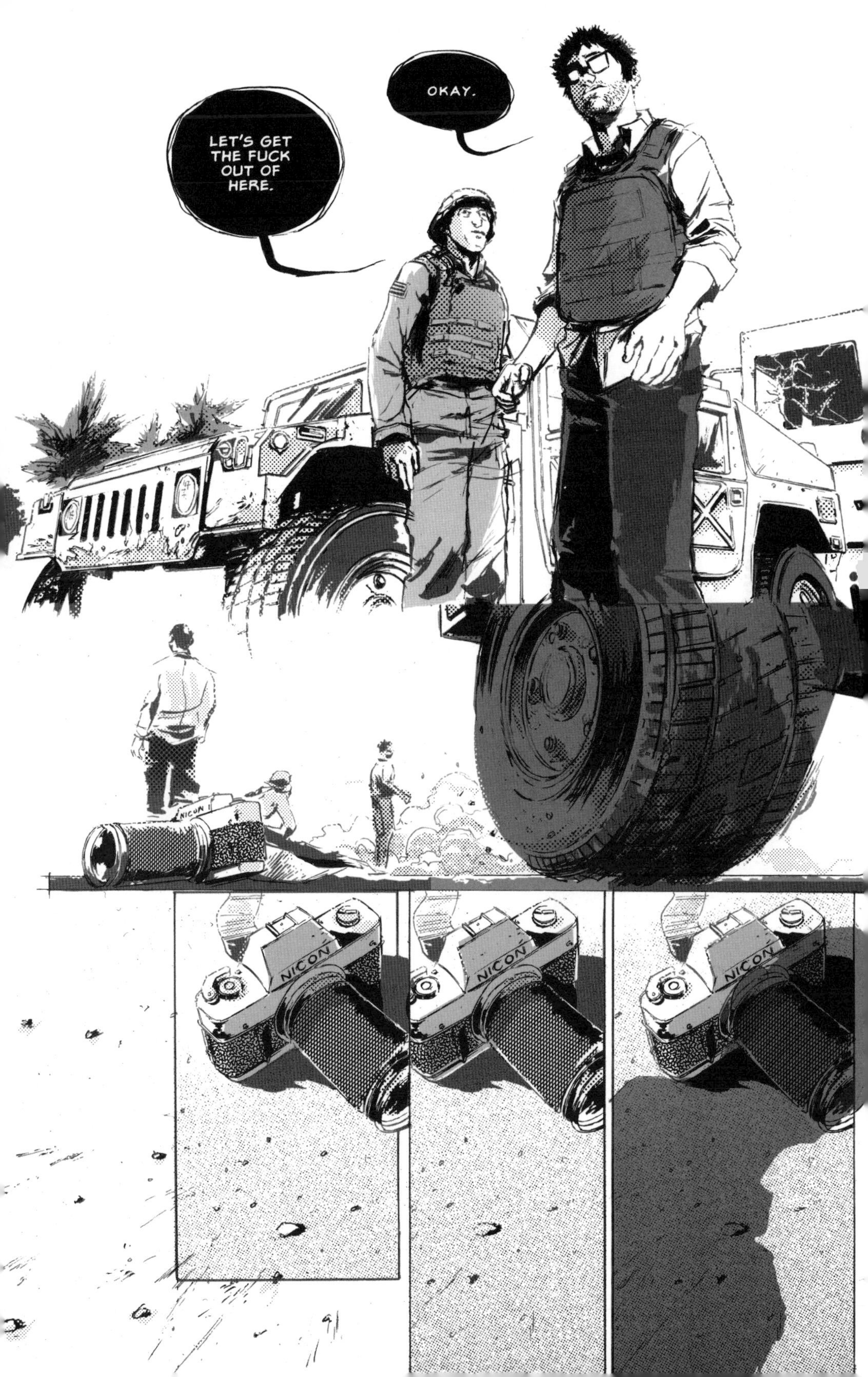
LET'S GET THE FUCK OUT OF HERE.
OKAY.
NICON
NICON
NICON
NICON

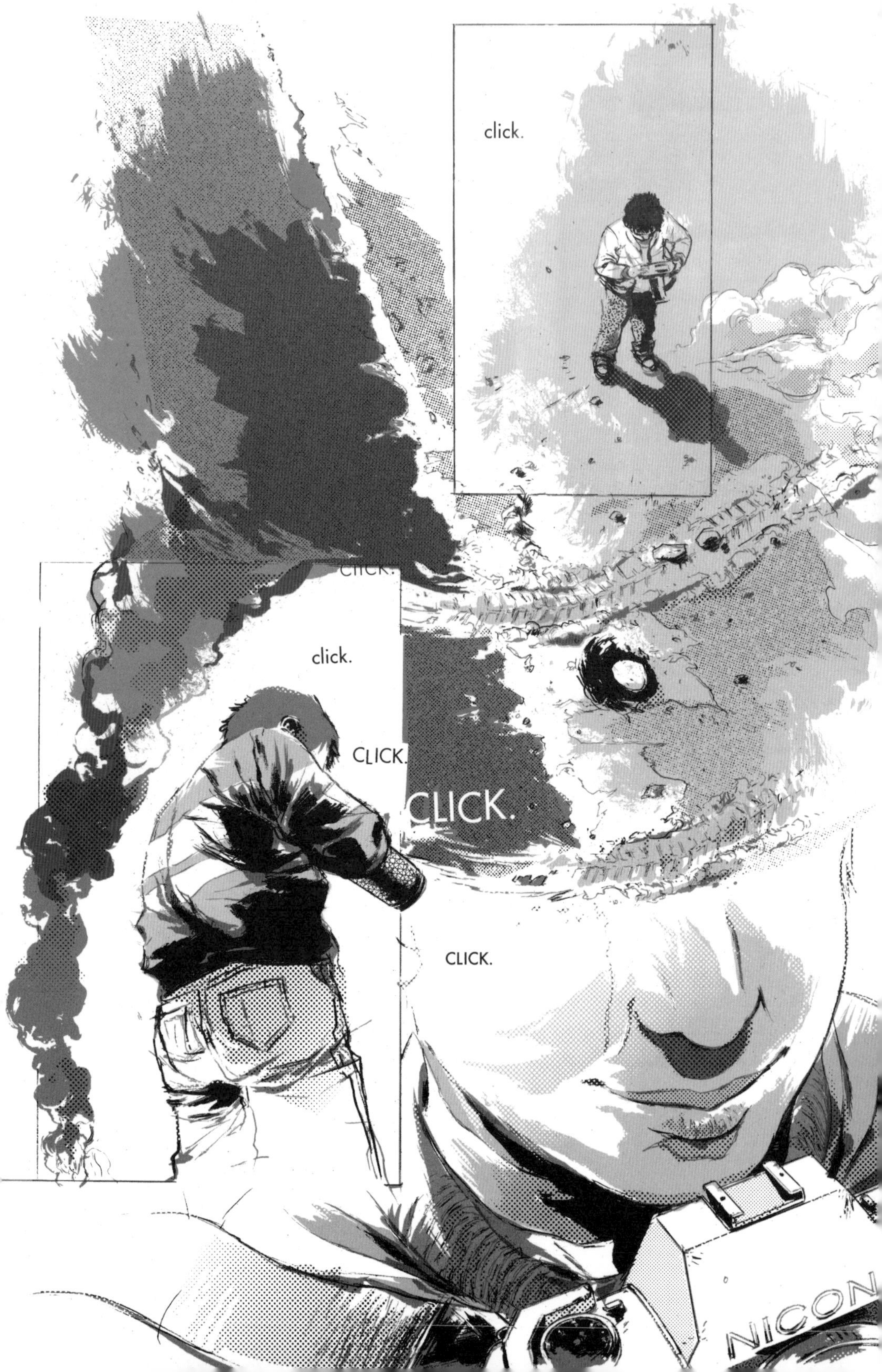
click.
click.
CLICK.
CLICK.
CLICK.
NICON

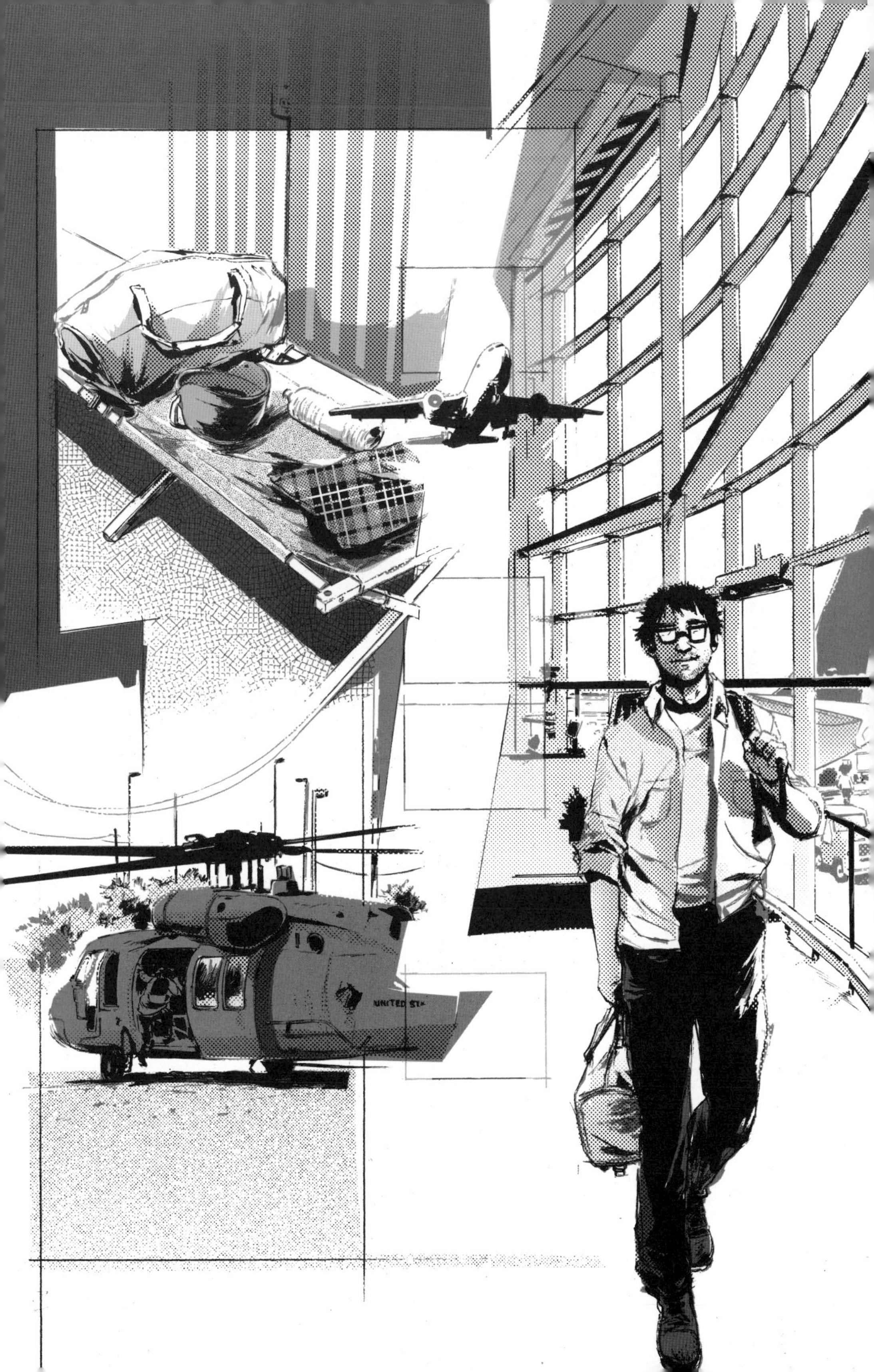
UNITED ST

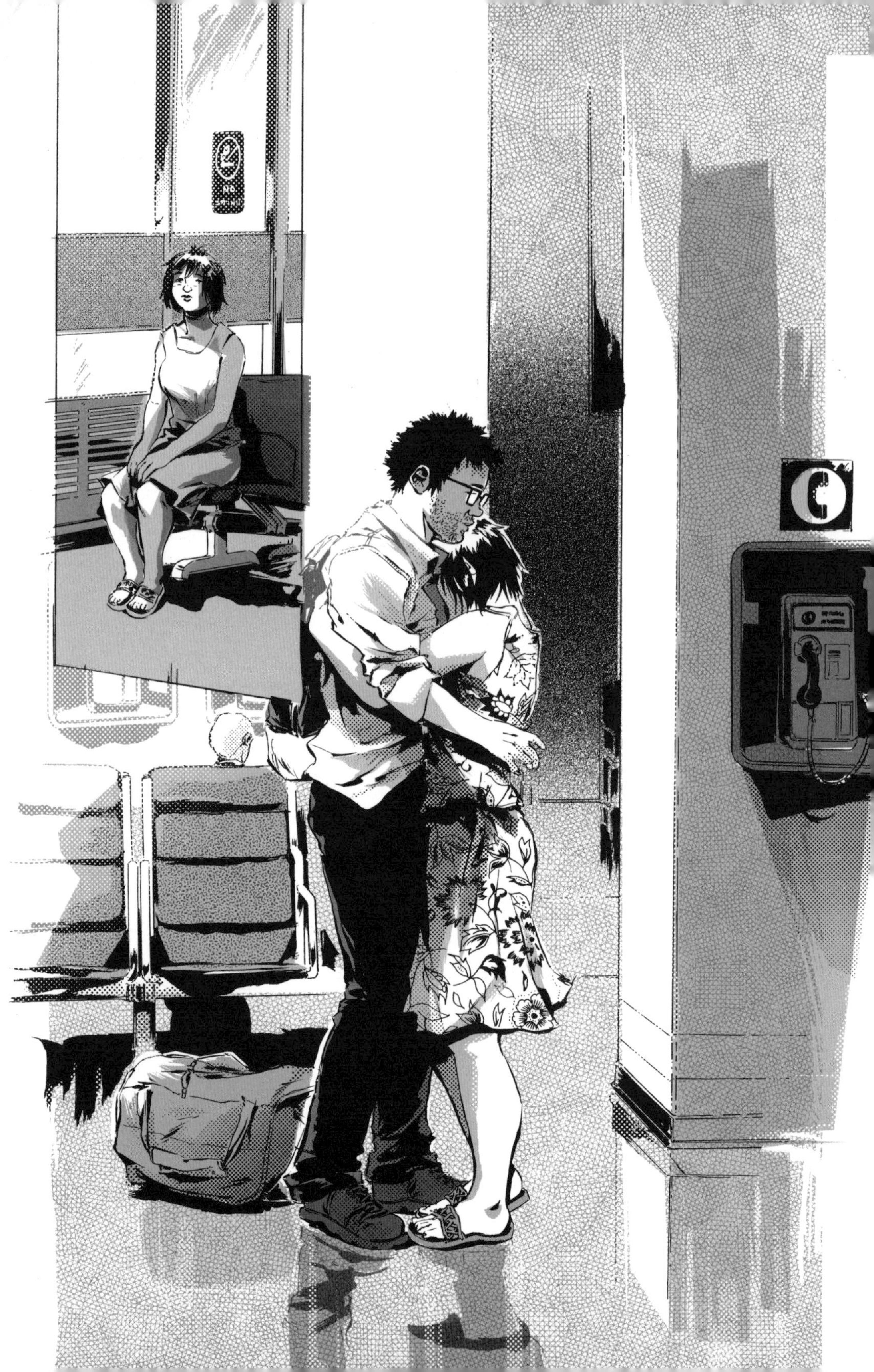

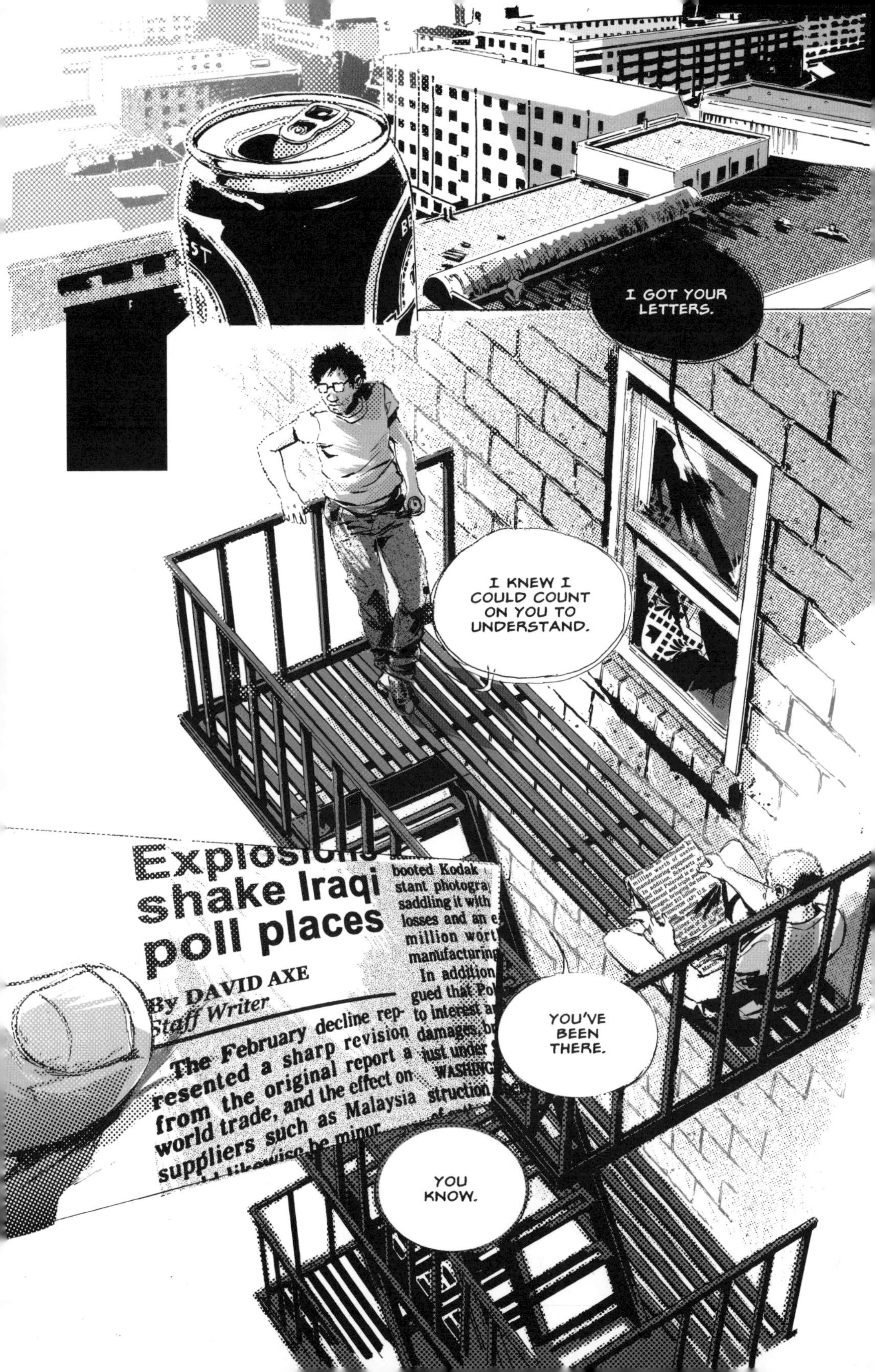
I GOT YOUR LETTERS.
I KNEW I COULD COUNT ON YOU TO UNDERSTAND.
Explosions
shake Iraqi
poll places
By DAVID AXE
Staff Writer
The February decline rep-
resented a sharp revision
from the original report a
world trade, and the effect on
suppliers such as Malaysia
booted Kodak
stant photogra
saddling it with
losses and an e
million wort
manufacturing
In addition
gued that Po
to interest a
damages, b
just under S
WASHING
struction
YOU'VE BEEN THERE.
YOU KNOW.

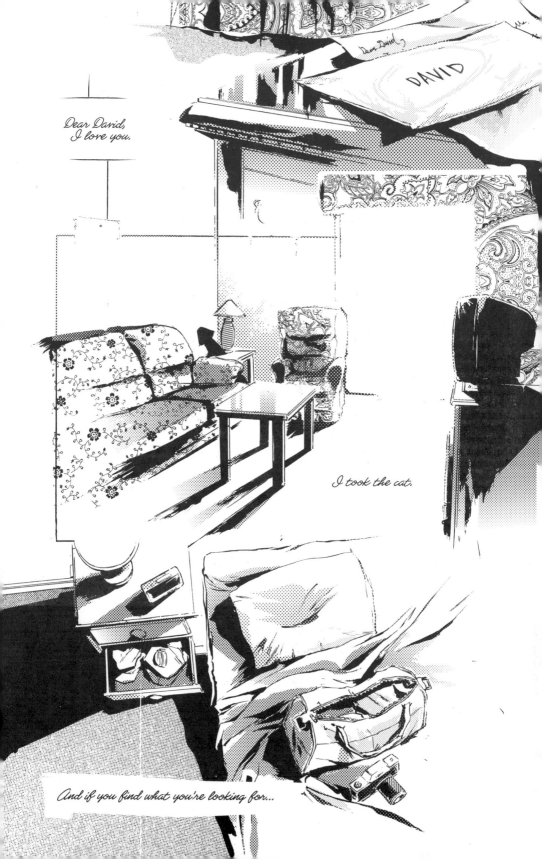

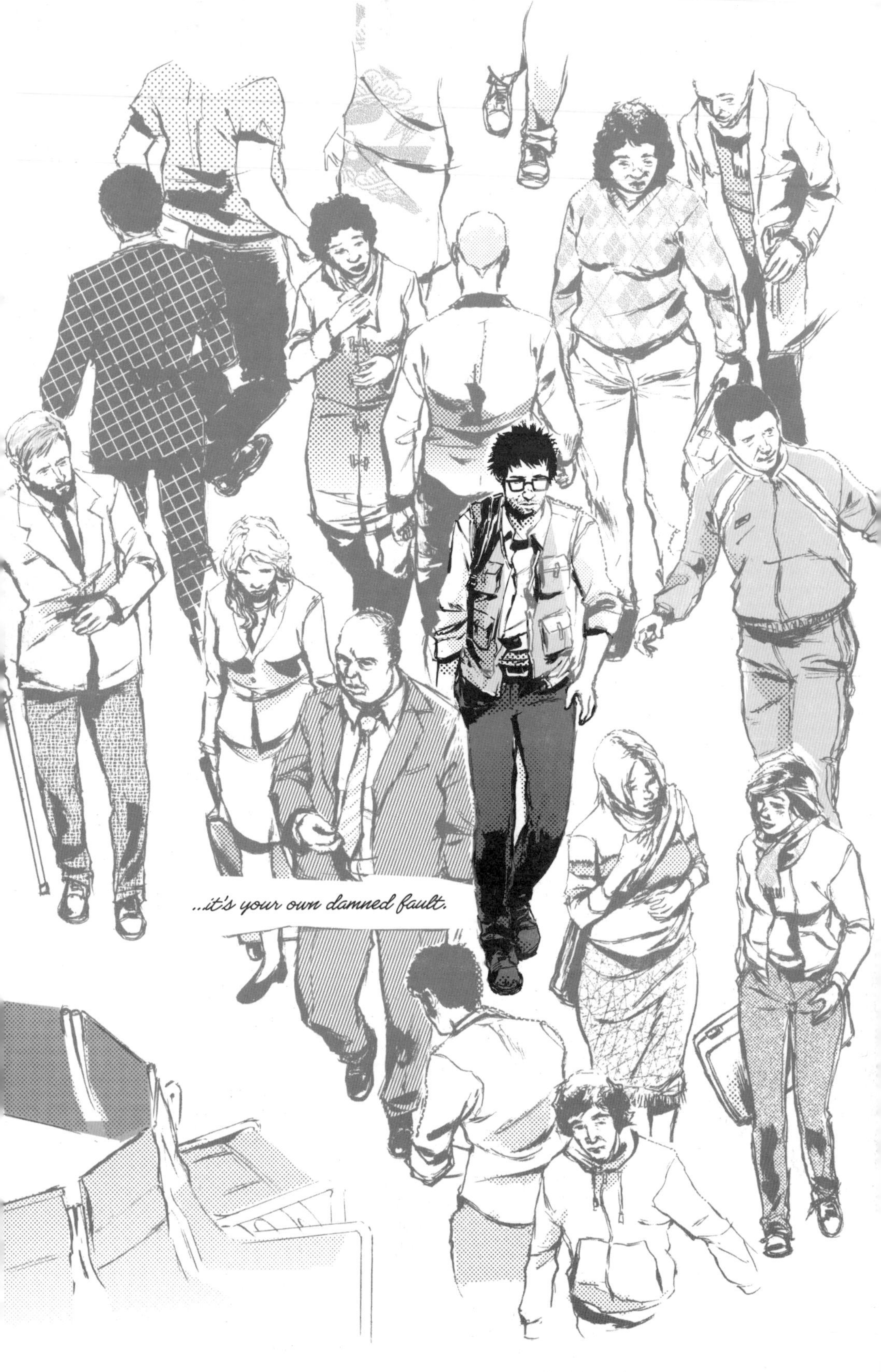
..it's your own damned fault.